KS3
Success

English

D1439537

Kath Jordan

Contents

Assessment

Reading fiction

Reading poetry

Reading non-fiction

Reading media texts

Writing

Shakespeare

Spelling, punctuation and grammar

Assessment at Key Stage 3

Types of Assessment

At the end of Key Stage 3, you will be awarded a National Curriculum Level. This is likely to be the product of a range of assessments. Your school may use the national **Optional Tests** for Years 7, 8 and 9 or they may have their **own tests**. Your school may also use **APP (Assessing Pupil Progress)**. This allows your teacher to assess your progress by reviewing your ongoing class work or through a specifically set assessment task.

The expected average level for students at the end of Key Stage 3 is Level 5 or 6.

This book covers Levels 4 – 7 and is designed to help you to achieve the best level you can regardless of the type of assessment used by your school. The questions at the end of each section will allow you to practise and develop important skills and provide useful preparation for the Optional Test or exams set by your school.

Attainment Targets

Attainment Target 1 – Speaking and Listening
Throughout Key Stage 3 you will learn and develop skills that will enable you to communicate more effectively. You will learn to speak confidently and fluently in a range of formal and informal situations. You will also explore a range of roles in group work including: contributing to, supporting and managing discussion. You will improve your listening skills and your ability to interpret tone of voice and gestures.

Attainment Target 2 – Reading
During your KS3 studies you will have the opportunity to read and respond to a range of texts: **plays, novels, poetry, non-fiction** and **media**. You will read modern texts and writing from other historical periods, including plays by **Shakespeare**. The skills you will develop are: **reading for meaning, understanding and responding to texts and understanding the author's craft**. You will have the opportunity to practise different reading techniques for different purposes.

Attainment Target 3 – Writing
Through your reading you will identify a range of techniques used to create particular effects in writing. You will learn to apply these techniques to make your own writing more effective. The major writing styles you will develop are: writing to **imagine, explore, entertain**; writing to **inform, explain, describe**; writing to **review, analyse** and **comment**; and writing to **persuade** or **argue**. You will also learn to **plan, draft** and **present** your work to make the most of the skills you have learned.

The Year 9 Optional Test

Your school may choose to use all or part of the Optional Test package to help decide on your end of Key Stage 3 Level. There are three test papers.

Reading Paper

Time: 1 hour plus 15 minutes reading time.

Assessment: Reading – understanding and response.

Tasks: You will be given a reading booklet containing three texts or extracts. The texts included will be a combination of fiction, non-fiction, media and poetry. In a separate booklet, you will be required to answer about 15 questions. The style of the questions will be varied but may include:
- ticking a box or writing a one word answer
- finding and copying a quotation and explaining why it is effective
- writing an extended answer, focusing on language and structure.

Writing Paper

Time: 1 hour and 15 minutes including planning time.

Assessment: Writing to: imagine, explore, entertain *or*
inform, explain, describe *or*
persuade, argue, advise *or*
analyse, review, comment.

Tasks: You will be required to complete two tasks that test your skills in two of the writing triplets listed above.

Task one is 45 minutes long and tests:
- sentence structure and punctuation
- text structure and organisation
- composition and effect.

Task two is 30 minutes long and tests:
- sentence and text organisation
- composition and effect
- spelling.

Shakespeare Paper

Time: 45 minutes

Assessment: Reading – understanding and response to Shakespeare

Tasks: You will be set a task which focuses on all or part of the set scenes from the Shakespeare play you have studied. The task you complete will be based on one of four areas of assessment: text in performance; character and motivation; language of the text; ideas, themes and issues.

Speaking and Listening

Your final level for *Speaking and Listening* is decided on by your English teacher. It is based on your performance over the whole of Key Stage 3.

How to improve your speaking and listening

Talking, discussing and sharing ideas are very useful ways to improve your understanding in other areas of English. Here are some ideas for improving your performance in some of the areas listed below.

Asking questions

This is an excellent way to improve your levels of understanding. Asking a question does not always mean that you don't understand what your teacher is talking about. If you do understand everything continue to ask questions. It allows you to look beneath the surface for less obvious meaning. You will be given credit for asking intelligent and searching questions.

Role play

Take time to think about the main concerns and emotions of the character you are taking on. Think about the **style** of language your character would use: formal or informal, local **slang** or **dialect**, etc.

Informal discussion

You will often be asked to discuss work in small groups (not just in English). It might be a poem, a character's strengths and weaknesses, a new approach to a problem or a social issue. The key to success is to speak and listen. This will allow you to share information and develop new ideas before sharing them with a larger group. You will lose marks if you remain silent and just listen. You will also lose marks if you are aggressive or you talk too much and ignore the ideas of others.

Answering questions

You should always attempt to answer questions in group **discussions** or oral tests. Even if you get the answer wrong, you will be given credit for thinking and trying your best. If you don't feel sure of an answer you should still have a go. You may have approached the problem from another angle or thought of something that your teacher did not consider. It does happen!

Reading aloud

This is a skill that can only be developed with practice. Always speak clearly and stand or sit up straight. Read to the punctuation to maintain the sense of what you are reading. Think about the content of the piece you are reading. Try to express the emotions of the characters you are reading by varying the **pace** and **tone** of your voice.

Formal debate

There are rules and procedures to follow in a **debate** – your teacher will explain these to you. The important thing to remember is that you must use **Standard English**. Do not use slang, colloquialisms or dialect words. A debate is about listening to others as well as putting your own point across. You will develop a much stronger argument if you listen and respond to the points made by the opposition. Make sure that you listen to their points and respond to them as well as putting forward your arguments.

To achieve Level 5 you need to

- **explain** ideas and feelings and make your **meaning explicit**
- **shape talk** in deliberate ways to **engage** the listener, including **adapting** vocabulary, grammar and non-verbal features
- **sustain** roles and responsibilities with **independence** in pairs and groups.

To move from Level 5 to Levels 6 and 7 you also need to

- **explore complex** ideas and feelings in a range of ways
- **organise talk** to guide the listener and demonstrate **empathy** and **understanding** through flexible choices of vocabulary, grammar and non-verbal features
- adopt a **range** of roles and responsibilities in group talk and **promote effective discussion**
- explore a **wide range** of subject matter with **precision** and **effect**
- **manage** and **manipulate** talk through apt choice of vocabulary, grammar and non-verbal features
- **sustain** effective **collaboration** and discussion in a range of group roles and responsibilities.

Tasks you might expect

- answering questions in class
- asking questions in class
- informal paired discussion
- informal group discussion
- formal debate
- formal paired interviews on a specified topic
- giving a talk (formal or informal)
- reading aloud
- role play or drama.

Have a go ...

1. Plan a talk on a subject you are interested in. Make a tape recording of your talk so you can work out how to improve your performance.
2. Choose a passage from your reading book and practise reading aloud at home.
3. Discuss your homework, the news or recent events in your favourite soap opera with a friend or your family.

KEY TERMS

Make sure you understand these terms before moving on!
- Standard English
- dialect
- debate
- slang
- pace
- tone
- style
- discussion

A glossary of literary terms

Use this *glossary* as you work through the following chapters in this book.

Imagery

Image: a 'picture' painted with words. Images can be developed from your five senses or they can be a description of a scene or an event.

Metaphor: an assertion that one object is a completely different object – there is no comparison made. Similar effect to **simile** but much more powerful, e.g. **His final words were icy splinters that lodged in her heart**.

Extended metaphor: a metaphor built up in a longer section of writing. The extended metaphor could be built using similes and other images.

Oxymoron: the joining of two words or phrases that appear to be complete opposites in meaning, e.g. **Feather of lead**, **bright smoke**, **cold fire**, **sick health**, **still waking sleep**. (*Romeo and Juliet* Act 1, Scene 1). This emphasises Romeo's dissatisfaction and confusion. He loves Rosaline, a Capulet; he should hate her.

Personification: an inanimate object is given human qualities or attributes. E.g. **Well-apparell'd April on the heel/Of limping winter treads** (*Romeo and Juliet* Act 1, Scene 2). This compares the seasons of spring and winter to a young lover and an old man near the end of his life.

Simile: a comparison of two distinctly different objects using the words **like** or **as**. Used to make particular associations in the mind of the reader, **e.g. snow covered the earth like a fluffy, white blanket.**

 Try to use the correct technical terms when you are writing about literature.

Device

These are some examples of **devices** you may encounter.

Alliteration: the repetition of a letter or letter sound at the beginning of a sequence of words. Used for emphasis and to link ideas. E.g. **The silver snake slithered silently by**.

Assonance: the repetition of identical or similar vowel sounds in a sequence of words. E.g. **Silent**, **quiet**, **light**, **time** (long 'i' sound).

Onomatopoeia: the sound of a word reflects the sound that it describes. E.g. **plop**, **hiss**, **fizz**, **splash**.

Structure

These are some examples of **structures** you may encounter.

Caesura: a pause in the middle of line of poetry or a sentence in prose, for dramatic effect, e.g. **We stood in silence, waiting; waiting for the explosion of anger we knew was coming**.

End-stopped line: in poetry, a full stop or colon at the end of a line that causes the reader to pause. This is sometimes used for dramatic effect, particularly when used with **enjambment**.

Enjambment: run-on lines – when the meaning of a line 'runs on' to the next line without any mark of punctuation. Often used to show movement or excitement in a poem.

Free verse: describes a poem that has a free structure, without a regular **rhythm**, **rhyme scheme** or **stanza** length.

Rhyme: the ending of one word sounds the same as another e.g. **late/fate**; **sight/might**; **health/wealth**.

- End rhymes are most common. These are rhymes which occur at the end of a verse line.
- Internal rhymes occur in the middle of a line.
- Rhyme schemes are patterns of rhyme within a poem. Used for a variety of effects: to give structure; in comic verse; to link ideas.

Rhythm: the pattern of beats or stresses in a line or group of lines.

Stanza: a verse – a group of lines in poetry.

 Don't just identify images or devices. You must explain why they are effective.

Other terms

Empathy: writers put themselves in the place of the person or object they are writing about; a stronger sensation than sympathy. If you empathise with someone you can understand how they feel and feel their pain, sadness, relief, etc. yourself.

Narrative: a story, whether told in prose or poetic form.

- First-person narrative: events are narrated by a person involved in the story, e.g. **I walked along the hard, stony ground**.
- Third-person narrative: events are narrated by an outside observer of the story, e.g. **He walked along the hard, stony ground**.

Narrator: the **storyteller**. Again you could have **first-** or **third-person narrators**.

Reading fiction

Fiction is stories describing imaginary events and people. Key ingredients in good fiction are:

- *plot*
- *relationships*
- *characterisation*
- *setting*
- use of language.

This section will help you to identify these elements and make a personal response to fictional texts.

Understanding fiction

To achieve Level 5 you need to:
- show some understanding of the feelings and behaviour of characters
- begin to read beneath the surface for meaning
- note the effect of particular words and phrases.

To move from Level 5 to Levels 6 and 7 you also need to:
- **support your ideas** about characters and relationships with **detailed reference to the text**
- write in some detail about the writer's **use of language** and the **structure** of the text
- comment on the **creation of setting and atmosphere**
- show **understanding** of the more **complex feelings** of the characters
- recognise what the writer is trying to achieve and how they do this
- trace the **development of plot, character, relationships** and **themes**
- give a **personal** and **critical response** to the text.

Plot

A well-constructed story-line will keep readers interested as they are keen to know how a story will develop. Many novels have sub-plots: minor story-lines that develop with the main plot. In a short extract it is only possible to work out what is happening at the time – you cannot comment on plot development.

Relationships

We all have relationships – with family, friends, teachers or work colleagues. To be believable, fictional characters must develop relationships within a text. The development of a relationship can often be the central element of the plot.

Characterisation

Writers try to know their characters very well – this helps to make them believable to the reader. We need to know what a character looks like; how they speak and behave; how they think and feel; how they get on with other characters. To maintain the flow of the plot it is not possible for a writer to directly tell us all of this information and so it is important to read beneath the surface for character development.

Setting

The setting of a piece of fiction, both in time and place, is very important. Setting can often be central to creating a particular atmosphere or reflecting the mood of a character.

 Remember to identify and explain the effective use of these elements.

Use of language

Interesting use of language is what makes us keep on reading. To comment on the use of language in fiction you need to recognise the use of particular devices and structures, and the extent of the detail and description. Effective use of language will ensure that all of the other elements are brought to life. When thinking about language in fiction you should consider:
- choice of vocabulary
- adjectives
- adverbs
- sentence structure
- imagery – simile, metaphor, personification, etc.

Basic questions

To help organise your thoughts, ask yourself four basic questions:
1. What is the story-line?
2. Who are the main characters?
3. What is their relationship?
4. Where is it set?

Make sure you understand these terms before moving on!
- fiction
- plot
- characterisation
- setting
- relationships

Example text

I'm the King of the Castle by Susan Hill

In this extract the boy, Kingshaw, has gone for a walk in the fields and has a very frightening experience.

Look for the ingredients:

- plot
- setting
- characterisation
- use of language
- relationships.

See pages 14 –15 where the text is explained.

The text 1

Extract from *I'm the King of the Castle* by Susan Hill

1 When he first saw the crow he took no notice. There had been several crows. This one glided into the corn on its **enormous, ragged black wings**. He began to be aware of it when it rose up suddenly, circled overhead, and then dived, to land not very far away from him. Kingshaw could see the feathers on its head, shining black in-between the butter-coloured cornstalks. Then it rose, and circled, and came down again, this time not quite landing, but flapping about his head, **beating its wings and making a sound like flat leather pieces being slapped together. It was the largest crow** he had ever seen. As it came down for the third time, he looked up and noticed its beak, opening in a screech. **The inside of its mouth was scarlet**, it had small glinting eyes.

2 Kingshaw got up and flapped his arms. For a moment, the bird retreated a little way off, and higher up in the sky. He began to walk rather quickly back, through the path in the corn, looking ahead of him. **Stupid to be scared of a rotten bird. What could a bird do?** But he felt his own extreme isolation, high up in the cornfield.

3 For a moment, he could only hear the soft thudding of his own footsteps, and the silky sound of the corn, brushing against him. Then there was a rush of air, as **the great crow** came beating down, and wheeled about his head. The beak opened and the hoarse caw came out again and again, from inside the **scarlet mouth**.

4 Kingshaw began to run, not caring, now, if he trampled the corn, wanting to get away, down into the next field. He thought that the corn might be some kind of crow's food store, in which he was seen as an invader. **Perhaps this was only the first of a whole battalion of crows, that would rise up and swoop at him.** Get on the grass then, he thought, get on to the grass, that'll be safe, it'll go away. He wondered if it had mistaken him for some hostile animal, lurking down in the corn.

Questions to ask yourself: What is the storyline? Who are the characters?

The text 2

5 His progress was very slow, through the cornfield, **the thick stalks bunched together and got in his way**, and he had to shove them back with his arms. But he reached the gate and climbed it, and dropped on to the grass of the field on the other side. Sweat was running down his forehead and into his eyes. **He looked up. The crow kept on coming. He ran.**

6 But it wasn't easy to run down this field, either, because of the tractor ruts. He began to leap wildly from side to side of them, his legs stretched as far as they could go, and for a short time, it seemed that he did go faster. The crow dived again, and, as it rose, **Kingshaw felt the tip of its black wing, beating against his face**. He gave a sudden, dry sob. Then his **left foot caught in one of the ruts** and he keeled over, going down straightforwards.

7 He lay with his face in the coarse grass, panting and sobbing by turns, with the **sound of his own blood pumping through his ears**. He felt the sun on the back of his neck, and his ankle was wrenched. But he would be able to get up. He raised his head, and wiped two fingers across his face. A streak of blood came off, from where a thistle had scratched him. He got unsteadily to his feet, taking in deep, desperate breaths of the close air. He could not see the crow.

8 But when he began to walk forwards again, it rose up from the grass a little way off, and began to circle and swoop. Kingshaw broke into a run, sobbing and wiping the damp mess of tears and sweat off his face with one hand. There was a blister on his ankle, rubbed raw by the sandal strap. The crow was still quite high, soaring easily, to keep pace with him. Now, he had scrambled over the third gate, and he was in the field next to the one that belonged to Warings. He could see the back of the house, he began to run much faster.

9 This time, he fell and lay completely winded. Through the runnels of sweat and the sticky tufts of his own hair, **he could see a figure looking down at him from one of the top windows of the house**.

10 Then, there was a single screech, and the terrible beating of wings, and the crow swooped down and landed in the middle of his back.

11 Kingshaw thought that, in the end, it must have been his screaming that frightened it off, for he dared not move. He lay and closed his eyes and felt the claws of the bird, digging into his skin, through the thin shirt, and began to scream in a queer, gasping sort of way. After a moment or two, the bird rose. He had expected it to begin pecking at him with its beak, **remembering terrible stories about vultures that went for living people's eyes**. He could not believe in his own escape.

Questions to ask yourself: What is the characters' relationship? Where is it set?

The text explained

- The writer is trying to create an *atmosphere* of tension and fear. To look at how this is achieved we should return to the basic elements of fiction described earlier.

  Story-line/*plot*: The boy, Kingshaw, is chased through a cornfield by a crow. He falls and the crow lands on his back. His screams finally scare it away.

  Characters/*relationship*: Kingshaw and the crow; hunter (crow) and hunted (Kingshaw).

  Setting: Isolated cornfields.

Plot

In this section the story is exciting and **dramatic**. It is a story of being chased or followed; it is told entirely from the victim's point of view so that the reader can identify closely with him. This section has a double build-up of tension. It builds up to paragraph 6 when the boy falls; we breathe a sigh of relief as the crow disappears. But then tension mounts when it reappears; there is a continued build-up to paragraph 9 when he falls again. This time it is worse because the crow lands on him.

Characterisation

- The **characterisation** of the boy is important because it helps us understand why he is so frightened. He obviously has a powerful imagination: 'Perhaps this was only the first of a whole battalion of crows,' (paragraph 4). He is also presented as being sensitive to what people say and quite easily frightened: 'remembering terrible stories about vultures that went for living people's eyes' (paragraph 11).
- 'Stupid to be scared of a rotten bird. What could a bird do?' The tone of this suggests that he is angry with himself for being scared. Although he seems to be quite young he is aware of his weaknesses and is critical of them.

Relationships

The relationship between hunter and hunted is developed through the boy's fear. The power of the crow is increased through reference to its size: 'enormous, ragged black wings'; 'the largest crow he had ever seen'; 'the great crow'. There really isn't a relationship as such and this makes the boy seem very isolated.

Setting

The setting is not the most important element in this piece of writing. The sense of menace is built up through the description of the crow rather than the surroundings. However, there is a sense that the landscape begins to turn against him: 'he felt his own extreme isolation'; 'thick stalks bunched together and got in his way'; 'it wasn't easy to run ... because of the tractor ruts'; 'a thistle had scratched him'.

Use of language

The way that this section is written, the use of language and **structure**, is what makes it powerful.

Detail There is extensive detail about the crow, making it seem more real. There is a description of what it sounds like as well as what it looks like. The detailed description of sounds made by the boy and the crow make the reader feel that there is a complete absence of background noise, highlighting his isolation: 'the sound of his own blood pumping through his ears.'

Structure The paragraphs in this extract are all quite short; this keeps the story moving at a quick pace. Some sentences are particularly short; this is a device used by writers to build up dramatic tension and suspense: 'He looked up. The crow kept on coming. He ran.'

Repetition Minor details become more significant because they are repeated. For example: 'the inside of its mouth was scarlet' (paragraphs 1 and 3). The structure is repetitive: he runs away and falls, then the same thing happens again.

Glossary Remember to refer to the glossary of literary terms on pages 8–9.

 A key point to think about is how the writer brings the crow to life.

KEY TERMS

Make sure you understand these terms before moving on!
- characterisation
- atmosphere
- detail
- structure
- repetition
- setting
- plot
- relationships

Fiction test

Use the questions to test your progress. Check your answers on page 94.

From *A Kestrel for a Knave* by Barry Hines
In this extract Mr Sugden is angry with Billy as he believes he let a goal in deliberately at the end of the PE lesson. Billy is made to have a shower before he is allowed to go home.

A Kestrel for a Knave

He thought this was funny, Billy didn't. So Sugden looked round for a more appreciative audience. But no-one was listening. They faced up for a few more seconds, then Billy turned back to his peg. He undressed quickly, bending his pumps free of his heels and sliding them off without untying the laces. When he stood up the black soles of his socks stamped damp imprints on the dry floor, which developed into a haphazard set of footprints when he removed his socks and stepped around pulling his jeans down. His ankles and knees were ingrained with ancient dirt which seemed to belong to the pigmentation of his skin. His left leg sported a mud stripe, and both his knees were encrusted. The surfaces of these mobile crusts were hair-lined, and with every flexion of the knee these lines opened into frown-like furrows.

For an instant, as he hurried into the showers, with one leg angled in running, with his dirty legs and huge rib cage moulding the skin of his white body, with his hollow cheek in profile, and the sabre of shadow emanating from the eye-hole, just for a moment he resembled an old print of a child hurrying towards the final solution.

****

While he worked on his ankles and heels Sugden stationed three boys at one end of the showers and moved to the other end, where the controls fed into the pipes on the wall … The blunt arrow was pointing to HOT. Sugden swung it back over WARM to COLD. For a few seconds there was no visible change in the temperature, and the red slice held steady, still dominating the dial. Then it began to recede, slowly at first, then swiftly, its share of the face diminishing rapidly.

The cold water made Billy gasp. He held out his hands as though testing for rain, then ran for the end. The three guards barred the exit.

'Hey up, shift! Let me out, you rotten dogs!' They held him easily so he swished back to the other end, yelling all the way along. Sugden pushed him in the chest as he clung his way round the corner.

'Got a sweat on, Casper?'

'Let me out, Sir. Let me come.'

'I thought you'd like a cooler after your exertions in goal.'

'I'm frozen!'

'Really?'

'Gi' o'er, Sir! It's not right!'

'And was it right when you let the last goal in?'

'I couldn't help it!'

'Rubbish, lad.'

Billy tried another rush. Sugden repelled it, so he tried the other end again. Every time he tried to escape the three boys bounced him back, stinging him with their snapping towels as he retreated. He tried manoeuvring the nozzles, but whichever way he twisted them the water still found him out. Until finally he gave up, and stood amongst them, tolerating the freezing spray in silence. When Billy stopped yelling the other boys stopped laughing, and when time passed and no more was heard from him, their conversations began to peter out, and attention gradually focused on the showers. Until only a trio was left shouting into each other's faces, unaware that the volume of noise in the room had dropped. Suddenly they stopped, looked round embarrassed, then looked towards the showers with the rest of the boys.

The cold water had cooled the air, the steam had vanished, and the only sound that came from the showers was the beat of water behind the partition; a mesmeric beat which slowly drew the boys together on the drying area. The boy guards began to look uneasy, and they looked across to their captain.

'Can we let him out now, Sir?'

'No!'

Glossary *The final solution:* During World War Two Hitler and the Nazis decided to kill all Jewish people. Often this was done by gassing in mass showers.

 Read the text; annotate the text; answer the questions.

❶ Look closely at the way the speech is punctuated in this extract. Which two punctuation marks are most often used to end sentences and what effect does this have?

Punctuation: (1 mark)

Explanation: (1 mark)

❷ Look closely at the section beginning 'For an instant...' Explain how this comparison creates sympathy for Billy. (3 marks)

❸ How does the writer show the boys' changing reaction to Billy and how does this increase our sympathy for him? Write your answer on a separate sheet.

Write about:
- what the boys do and say
- the language used to describe their behaviour
- the difference between Mr Sugden and the boys. (6 marks)

Reading poetry

By the end of this section you will be able to identify and comment on:

- title
- poetic voice
- imagery
- language devices
- *structure.*

You should be able to use these elements to make a *personal response* to *poetry*.

Reading the poem

- You shouldn't expect to fully understand everything about a poem after a first reading; it might be packed full of **emotions**, ideas and **images**. Reading a poem involves detective work – you often have to look closely under the surface for clues.
- Try reading a poem through three times, each time looking for a different set of clues.

  First reading: the general meaning and story-line of the poem (if it has one).

  Second reading: feelings and emotions contained in the poem.

  Third reading: interesting images contained in the poem.

Understanding a poem

To achieve Level 5 you need to:

- begin to look for layers of meaning beneath the surface of the text
- understand ideas and feelings in the poem
- notice the effects of particular words and phrases.

To move from Level 5 to Levels 6 and 7 you also need to:

- comment on the effective use of words and phrases and particular devices of language
- locate and comment on the use of imagery
- comment on the structure of the poem
- trace development within a poem
- give a personal response to the poem and what you think the poet has achieved.

What to expect

- Many students think they 'can't do poetry' – they worry about it, perhaps because it is less familiar than other forms of writing. We feel comfortable with fiction, advertising and newspaper reports because we see them around us all the time.
- When trying to understand poetry, it is important to remember that it is simply another means of communicating. A poem is written by another human being wanting to communicate ideas, feelings, memories, hopes and dreams. It may seem less obvious than other forms of writing but this is just because poems are often more compact and less expansive than fiction, for example.

Glossary

As you work through this section remember to refer to the glossary of literary terms on pages 8–9.

Have a go ...

Now read the poem by Vernon Scannell printed on the next page. Read it three times and look for the different clues each time. See if you agree with the ideas on the following page.

Remember, just like a painting or a piece of music, a poem can be responded to in many different ways. So long as you can justify (back up and explain) your opinion, you can't go wrong!

Make sure you understand these terms before moving on!

- poetry
- emotions
- images
- personal response
- structure

KEY TERMS

Example text

Hide and Seek *meaning? / is it just a game?*

Call out. Call loud: "I'm ready! Come and find me!" *← voice*
The sacks in the toolshed smell like the seaside. *sensory detail*
They'll never find me in this salty dark,
But be careful that your feet aren't sticking out.
Wiser not to risk another shout.
The floor is cold.They'll probably be searching
The bushes, near the swing. Whatever happens
You mustn't sneeze when they come prowling in.
And here they are, whispering at the door;
You've never heard them sound so hushed before.

use of punctuation / sensory detail

Don't breathe. Don't move. Stay dumb. Hide in your
    blindness.
They're moving closer, someone stumbles, mutters;
Their words and laughter scuffle and they're gone.
But don't come out just yet; they'll try the lane,
And then the greenhouse and back here again.
They must be thinking that you're very clever,
Getting more puzzled as they search all over.
It seems a long time since they went away.

sensory detail

Your legs are stiff, the cold bites through your coat; *← personification*
The dark damp smell of sand moves in your throat.
It's time to let them know that you're the winner.
Push off the sacks. Uncurl and stretch. That's better!
Out of the shed and call to them "I've won!

personification

Here I am! Come and own up I've caught you!" *voice*
The darkening garden watches. Nothing stirs.
The bushes hold their breath; the sun is gone.
Yes, here you are. But where are they who sought you?

use of punctuation

Vernon Scannell

💡 *Making notes or annotating a poem (underlining and highlighting, etc.) is a helpful way of organising your thoughts about it.*

First reading

The poem is about a young child playing hide and seek. He waits excitedly in a dark shed, hoping he will not be found. He hears his friends looking for him but they go away without finding him. After hiding for a long time, the child comes out of the shed to celebrate his victory but discovers that his friends have all gone home and left him.

Second reading

Excitement and anticipation; discomfort; victory; disappointment and confusion; isolation.

Third reading

"salty dark"; "hide in your blindness"; "their words and laughter scuffle"; "the bushes hold their breath".

Title: Hide and Seek

The **title** of this poem suggests childhood fun, innocence and excitement and this is the mood created at the beginning of the poem. However, as the poem progresses, there is some suggestion that rather than being a fun game between friends, something slightly more sinister is being described. At the end of the poem the boy is left in complete isolation and gathering darkness – even "the sun is gone" – as his friends have abandoned the game and abandoned him.

There are some clues earlier in the poem that the game is not as innocent as it first appears – the other children are described as "prowling" and later there is a sense of creeping anxiety, "It seems a long time since they went away".

Personification

Personification is used several times in the poem often to create a slightly sinister effect. When the boy has been waiting for a long time to be found and is becoming very uncomfortable in the shed, the cold is described as biting through his coat as if he is under attack. At the end of the poem "the darkening garden watches" and "the bushes hold their breath". This gives the impression that there is perhaps something lurking in the darkness waiting for the boy who has been abandoned by his friends.

Make sure you understand these terms before moving on!
■ Personification   ■ Title   ■ Annotation

The text explained

Sensory images

A **sensory image** draws on one or more of your five senses (touch, taste, smell, sight and hearing). There are a number of sensory images in the poem: the sacks which "smell like the seaside", "the salty dark", "hide in your blindness". They are used to create a sense of immediacy – to give the reader the feeling of actually experiencing the same things as the boy in the poem. Sometimes they are used to trigger our own "sensory memories" – the "smell of the seaside" is likely to remind all adults of their childhood.

Sensory images are particularly suitable for a poem about childhood. Children learn through their senses and new sights, sounds and smells are often remembered.

Sometimes a number of senses are combined to create a very powerful image. A good example of this is "The dark damp smell of sand moves in your throat". Here the combination of ideas linked to touch, smell, sight and taste create a powerful sense of the boy being completely closed in and almost choked by his experience in the shed. It is an unpleasant image and hints at the growing anxiety the boy feels as he continues to wait to be discovered.

Poetic voice

The poem is written almost entirely in the second person: "Be careful that your feet aren't sticking out". Together with the immediacy of the sensory images this allows the reader to feel that they could actually be the child hiding in the shed. This means that the reader has a stronger connection with the emotions of excitement and anticipation at the beginning of the poem and shares the gnawing sense of anxiety and doubt that creeps in the longer the child stays undiscovered.

The final line of the poem seems like a direct address to the child forcing him to confront the fact he has been abandoned. "Yes, here you are, but where are they who sought you?"

At two points in the poem, the voice of the child is represented directly. These lines are presented in speech marks to indicate the child's excited shouts: "I'm ready! Come and find me!"

Use of punctuation

Poetry does not follow the same rules as prose. It does not have to be written in sentences. Therefore, the use of punctuation in a poem can be very revealing. The poet uses punctuation to create effects rather than for grammatical accuracy.

In the line "Don't breathe. Don't move. Stay dumb." or each instruction is separated by a full stop. The full stops act as caesuras and give emphasis to each pair of words, creating a sense of breathless excitement as the child is desperate not to be discovered. In contrast, the lines that follow form a much longer 'sentence'.

The final line of the poem is a question. The use of the question mark at the end of the poem creates a lingering sense of doubt about where the boy's friends have gone. Did they get bored of looking and give up? Did they know where he was all along and deliberately and cruelly abandon him? Did they get distracted and genuinely forget about him?

Structure and form

The poem is written in one long stanza but it is given **structure** by the clear narrative and references to time that run through it. It doesn't have a regular rhythm or rhyme scheme and some lines are shorter than others. There are some **rhyming couplets** which add emphasis to certain ideas.

The most interesting use of rhyme comes at the end of the poem. The child's words "caught you" are rhymed with the poet's final words "sought you". This creates a direct link between the child's victorious shout when he thinks he's won the game and the poet's question which emphasises the child's isolation at the end of the poem.

Advice

Go back to the poem and the explanations and pick out the parts you feel most comfortable with, then try to look for those elements in other poems that you read. Build up gradually, looking for different elements each time you read.

The basic areas covered are:

- title
- imagery
- language devices
- poetic voice
- structure
- personal response

KEY TERMS

Make sure you understand these terms before moving on!

- Sensory image
- Poetic voice
- Rhyming couplets
- Structure

Poetry test

Use the questions to test your progress. Check your answers on page 94.

Nettles

My son aged three fell in the nettle bed.
'Bed' seemed a curious name for those green spears,
That regiment of spite behind the shed:
It was no place for rest. With sobs and tears
The boy came seeking comfort and I saw
White blisters beaded on his tender skin.
We soothed him till his pain was not so raw.
At last he offered us a watery grin,
And then I took my billhook, honed the blade
And went outside and slashed in fury with it
Till not a nettle in that fierce parade
Stood upright any more. And then I lit
A funeral pyre to burn the fallen dead,
But in two weeks the busy sun and rain
Had called up tall recruits behind the shed:
My son would often feel sharp wounds again.

Vernon Scannell

Glossary *Billhook*: a traditional cutting tool with wooden handle and metal blade used for cutting down shrubs etc.

 Read the poem three times and make notes. Annotate the poem. Answer the questions.

1st READING
The story-line

....

....

....

2nd READING
Feelings and emotions in the poem

....

....

....

3rd READING
Interesting images and phrases

....

....

....

....

PRACTICE QUESTIONS

❶ Find and copy a metaphor used in the poem and explain why it is effective.

Metaphor:

Explanation: (2 marks)

❷ How does the poet use the phrase "watery grin" to show how his son is feeling?
                                                                          (2 marks)

❸ Explain how the images of war used in the poem help to show how the poet is feeling. You should make reference to exact words and phrases used in the poem. (You may need to answer on a separate sheet)   (5 marks)

Reading a non-fiction text

Some *non-fiction* texts you might expect to study during Key Stage 3 are:

- *instruction*
- *information*
- *persuasion*
- *recount*
- *explanation*
- *discursive.*

Understanding non-fiction

To achieve Level 5 you need to:
- understand the **purpose** of a text
- identify **key features, themes** and **characters** in a text
- **select sentences, phrases** and **relevant information** to support your views
- **collect** and **collate** information from different sources.

To move from Level 5 to Levels 6 and 7 you also need to:
- identify different **layers of meaning**
- comment on the **significance** and **effect of different devices**, including layout where appropriate
- **summarise** a range of information from **different sources**
- show **understanding** of the way information is conveyed in a range of texts
- **select** and **analyse** information and ideas
- give a **personal response** to the text.

Instruction

Purpose: to instruct how something should be done through a series of sequenced steps.

Structure a statement of what is to be achieved
list of materials and equipment
sequenced/chronological steps
sometimes a diagram or illustration.

Language written in the imperative – tells you what to do.

Information

Purpose: to describe the way things are; to give information.

Structure information is clearly organised
information is linked
examples are included.

Language present tense
written in the third person: he, she, it.

Persuasion

Purpose: to persuade or to argue the case for a point of view.

Structure opening statement: e.g. vegetables are good for you

persuasive argument – point plus support

summary of argument and restatement of opening.

Language present tense

logical connectives.

Recount

Purpose: to retell events.

Structure an opening which sets the scene

events are retold in chronological order.

Language written in the past tense

uses temporal connectives: then, next, after

focuses on individuals or groups of people: I, we.

Explanation

Purpose: to explain the process involved in natural and social phenomena or to explain how something works.

Structure a statement to introduce the topic

a series of logical steps explaining how and why something happens

steps continue until explanation is complete.

Language present tense

logical connectives: this shows, because

temporal connectives: then, next, later.

Discursive

Purpose: to present arguments and information from differing viewpoints.

Structure statement of the issue to be discussed

argument for, plus supporting evidence

argument against, plus supporting evidence

summary of arguments and recommendation.

Language present tense

logical connectives: therefore, however.

KEY TERMS

Make sure you understand these terms before moving on!
- non-fiction
- recount
- discursive
- explanation
- information
- persuasion
- instruction
- purpose

 These conventions are not a rigid set of rules – they are intended as a guide.

Reading non-fiction

The kind of non-fiction texts that you might expect to find in your test are:

- *Autobiography*
- *Diaries*
- *Biography*
- *Letters*
- *Travel writing*
- Media – including newspapers, magazines and web pages

In this section you will find a brief explanation about why they are written and what to look for in each.

Based on fact

A non-fiction text is something that is **based** on **fact** or involves a true story. However, the boundaries between fiction and non-fiction are becoming more and more blurred. There have always been historical novels to read but now we are able to watch 'docu-dramas' on television and new words like 'faction' and 'news fiction' have become commonplace media terms.

Autobiography

A personal life story. The author selects and reconstructs events from their own life to share with the public. We should remember when reading an autobiography that no-one has total recall of their entire life and a personal account of the subject's own life is bound to be **biased**. The events from a person's past are, of course, recounted with hindsight, allowing us to see the lessons that have been learned from those events.

Biography

A written account of a person's life, written by someone else. There are two kinds of biography: authorised and unauthorised.

Authorised

An authorised biographer has the permission of the subject to write their life story. Often the biographer will have been asked by the subject to write about them and may have spent many hours discussing the events to be included. This will affect the way they recount particular events.

Unauthorised

Unauthorised biographies are written without the permission of the subject. They are generally thought to be less reliable. The biographer relies on information from people who know the subject and from more widely available sources. Some might claim that this kind of biography could be more accurate, as the writer is under no obligation to hide anything that could be embarrassing or damaging.

Diaries

Maybe you keep a diary or a journal. Would you like thousands of people to read it? Diaries are a record of personal thoughts, feelings, hopes and dreams. One of the most famous and widely read diaries is that of Anne Frank. Her father allowed its publication after her death in a concentration camp. Her writings have been an inspiration to people all over the world. When we read a diary we should always remember that it is an intensely personal document, not at all like a biography that was always intended for publication.

Letters

Like diaries, private letters are personal documents not initially intended for publication. Public letters, written for newspapers or widespread circulation are, of course, very different and may aim to persuade us of something or change our opinions.

Travel writing

Although people have long been fascinated with travel, travel writing is a newly popular genre. It is as much about people and personal struggle as it is about the places they have travelled to. Travel writing is often designed to entertain as well as inform. This form of writing can be compared with diaries, as accounts of journeys often begin as personal journals.

Biased text

Remember that texts written by one person about their own personal experiences are bound to be **biased**. Some elements may be given more emphasis whilst others are hardly mentioned. As you develop your understanding of non-fiction texts, **a key skill will be the ability to recognise when you, as a reader, are being manipulated**. It is important to try to keep the facts in mind, to take a balanced view and to work out exactly what the writer wants you to think and feel. As you improve your reading skills you will find it easier to do this and to see how and why a writer achieves his or her aims.

Basic questions

When you read a non-fiction text, begin by asking yourself four basic questions.

Who is it aimed at?
Why has it been written?
What is the main idea/message in the text?
How is that message put across?

Media

See Media section on pages 36–45.

KEY TERMS

Make sure you understand these terms before moving on!

- autobiography
- biography
- travel writing
- letter
- diary
- bias
- fact

Example text

This extract is from Nelson Mandela's autobiography *Long Walk to Freedom*. He writes about his rural African upbringing; his struggle against apartheid; his imprisonment and finally his election as President of South Africa. This extract is from the section entitled 'Robben Island: the dark years'. In it he describes his prison life.

Look for the conventions of recount:

- retells events in chronological order
- uses temporal connectives
- written in the past tense
- focuses on individuals or identified groups.

See pages 32–33 where the text is explained.

The text

Long Walk to Freedom

In the midst of breakfast, the guards would yell, "Val in! Val in!" (Fall in! Fall in!), and we would stand outside our cells for inspection. Each prisoner was required to have the three buttons of his khaki jacket properly buttoned. We were required to doff our hats as the warder walked by. If our buttons were undone, our hats unremoved, or our cells untidy, we were charged with a violation of the prison code and punished with either solitary confinement or the loss of meals.

After inspection we would work in the courtyard hammering stones until noon. There were no breaks; if we slowed down the warders would yell at us to speed up. At noon, the bell would clang for lunch and another metal drum of food would be wheeled into the courtyard. For Africans, lunch consisted of boiled mealies, that is, coarse kernels of corn. The Indians and Coloured prisoners received samp, or mealie rice, which consisted of ground mealies in a soup-like mixture. The samp was sometimes served with vegetables, whereas our mealies were served straight.

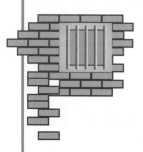

For lunch we often received phuzamandla, which means 'drink of strength', a powder made from mealies and a bit of yeast. It is meant to be stirred into water or milk, and when it is thick it can be tasty, but the prison authorities gave us so little of the powder that it barely coloured the water. I would usually save my powder for several days until I had enough to make a proper drink, but if the authorities discovered you were hoarding food, the powder was confiscated and you were punished.

Questions to ask yourself: Who is it aimed at? Why has it been written?

After lunch we worked until 4, when the guards blew shrill whistles and we once again lined up to be counted and inspected. We were then permitted half an hour to clean up. The bathroom at the end of our corridor had two seawater showers, a saltwater tap and three large galvanized metal buckets, which were used as bathtubs. There was no hot water. We would stand or squat in these buckets, soaping ourselves with the brackish water, rinsing off the dust from the day. To wash yourself with cold water when it is cold outside is not pleasant, but we made the best of it. We would sometimes sing while washing, which made the water seem less icy. In those early days, this was one of the only times when we could converse.

Precisely at 4.30 there would be a loud knock on the wooden door at the end of the corridor, which meant that supper had been delivered. Common-law prisoners used to dish out the food to us and we would return to our cells to eat it. We again received mealie pap porridge, sometimes with the odd carrot or piece of cabbage or beetroot thrown in – but one usually had to search for it. If we did get a vegetable, we would usually have the same one for weeks on end, until the cabbage or carrots were old and mouldy and we were thoroughly sick of them. Every other day we received a small piece of meat with our porridge. The meat was mostly gristle.

For supper, Coloured and Indian prisoners received a quarter loaf of bread (known as katkopf, that is, a cat's head, after the shape of the bread) and a slab of margarine. Africans, it was presumed, did not care for bread as it was a 'European' type of food.

Typically, we received even less than the scanty amounts stipulated in the regulations. This was because the kitchen was rife with smuggling. The cooks – all of whom were common-law prisoners – kept the best food for themselves or their friends. Often they would lay aside the tastiest morsel for the warders in exchange for favours or preferential treatment.

At 8 p.m. the night warder would lock himself in the corridor with us, passing the key through a small hole in the door to another warder outside. The warder would then walk up and down the corridor, ordering us to go to sleep. No cry of 'lights out' was ever given on Robben Island because the single mesh-covered bulb in our cell burned day and night. Later, those studying for higher degrees were permitted to read until 10 or 11 p.m.

Questions to ask yourself: What is the main idea or message? How is that message put across?

The text explained

This description of daily routine is used to show that basic human rights were only just attended to in this prison. It also clearly shows that the system was run on prejudice. That is the main message of the text – now we need to look more closely at how it is put across to the reader.

The text explained

Who?   It is aimed at people interested in politics; apartheid and the struggle against it; general interest, Mandela being a well-known figure around the world.

What?   The harshness of the regime; prejudice in the prison; that it is possible to survive such hardship with dignity.

Why?   To maintain the author's sense of identity in times of trouble (much of it was written whilst still in prison). To make people aware of the struggle against apartheid and how people suffered. To make sure people don't forget how things were and to ensure more progress is made.

How?   A factual and detailed account told without emotion; comparisons of food to highlight prejudice.

Relationships

The writer has used this book as a way of communicating with others. This extract shows that communication with other prisoners was rare: 'In those early days, this was one of the only times we could converse.' This extract also shows that relationships with the guards were poor: 'In the midst of breakfast, ... "Val in! Val in!"'; 'the guards blew shrill whistles'; 'a loud knock on the wooden door'; 'ordering us to go to sleep'. All of these quotations show that there was no conversation between prisoners and guards, just the shouting of orders.

Sanitation

Arrangements for washing are described in great detail, again done to highlight how poor the conditions were.

Routine

There are many references to time in this extract and meals are described in great detail. This indicates the daily routine was important, perhaps for keeping track of time. It also shows that there was little of interest happening on normal days. Does the writer find routine a comfort?

Food

All of the prison meals are described in detail. Each time there is a description of the differences in rations for Black prisoners and Coloured and Indian prisoners. This is done to highlight prejudice in the system. 'The samp was sometimes served with vegetables, whereas our mealies were served straight.'

 All of these comments are backed up with direct quotation or close reference to the text.

Coping strategies

There are some clues in this extract as to how the prisoners coped with the harsh regime. They are to do with communication and stimulating the brain: 'We would sometimes sing while washing, which made the water seem less icy.'

Tone

Although the writer is describing a 'dark time' in his life, the **tone** is very matter-of-fact and not at all self-pitying or exaggerated. This makes the reader more inclined to believe that the details are true and the harshness of his existence has not been dramatised for impact.

Punishment

In this extract punishments are not described but it is made clear that minor offences are punished severely: 'If our buttons were undone ... punished with either solitary confinement or the loss of meals.'

Recount text conventions

Autobiographies follow many of the **text conventions** of a recount:

- retells events in **chronological** order: this extract details a day in prison from breakfast to bedtime
- uses temporal **connectives**: 'after inspection ...', 'at 8 p.m...'
- written in past tense: 'for lunch we often received'
- focuses on individuals or identified groups: 'the guards would yell', 'we worked until 4'.

KEY TERMS

Make sure you understand these terms before moving on!
- chronological
- tone
- text convention
- connectives

Non-fiction test

Use the questions to test your progress. Check your answers on page 94.

This extract is from a piece of travel writing *On Foot Through Africa* by Ffyona Campbell. Here she describes part of her journey through Zaire. Villagers were often hostile, fearing that she was involved in the slave trade. Although she made the journey alone and on foot, she did have two back-up drivers, Bill and Blake, who feature in this passage.

On Foot Through Africa

1 I was the constant focus of their attention. The boys went ahead through one village and I passed along ten minutes later to find the people still standing together in the centre staring after them. I came behind them, a white, undefended, feeling like a beetle walking into a dawn patrol of ants. An old man broke the silence with a barrage of shrill words. The crowd broke and re-formed around me, their shrill whooping getting louder and louder until it was a throbbing wall of sound. I daren't turn. I walked out of the village and I waved goodbye. Ten minutes later the hill behind was teeming with bands of children, whooping and hollering, their demands growing louder and louder. The tension needed relieving so I turned and smiled. They closed around me, getting excited. The ringleader grabbed at my necklace, demanding to know what it was.

2 'It is a present from my husband,' I said. 'Thank you for escorting me to him – he is waiting ahead.' And luckily both of them were.
Getting into camp was a relief not just because it meant I was safe but because I was not the only thing they were baiting any more.

3 A couple of the boys would arrive first to watch the camp from a distance. Then more would come, just standing a small distance away. As the group grew, they merged into a crowd and became cocky. They were kids who'd found a new toy, and they loved to bait, to mess about with it to see what it would do. They did this to me on the road – imitating me, shouting at me, and then a stone would be thrown. Blake had to diffuse this in camp; I had to defuse this on the road. In camp, we could usually get them to leave in the early stages by picking out one and staring at him – this made them very self-conscious and they'd turn and leave.

4 On the road, I would turn and suddenly growl with my hands out like claws. The children would scatter like impala changing direction. Some would take a look back at a distance when they saw me laughing, they would laugh too and run back to hold my hand and dance along. But, after a short while, they wanted to do it again – as kids do – and the group would be gradually replaced as I walked through a long village, kids getting bored with it and falling back, to be replaced with new ones who started the baiting again.

5 The young teenage girls were the worst – they imitated my gait and would not respond to my games or return my smiles; they just sniggered. Teenage girls are the same the world over. There were times when I couldn't get the kids to laugh, possibly because I wasn't exuding the right presence. Then the stoning would be vicious. It is humiliating to be stoned, to be physically and symbolically chased out. I couldn't run; I couldn't stop them by stoning them back; I couldn't reason with them; I couldn't often get the adults to help. I was crying inside. Sometimes they hollered like Red Indians, a disorientating sound that made me feel like a hunted animal. I wondered if it was, indeed, a form of hunting. I hummed a Vangelis tune to make me feel like I wasn't actually there, just watching myself in a movie.

💡 *Read the text. Annotate the text. Answer the questions.*

Who?	Why?	What?	How?

❶ Find and copy a simile in the first paragraph. Explain why it is effective.

Simile:

Explanation: (3 marks)

❷ In the final paragraph, the phrase 'I couldn't' is repeated
several times in one sentence. What is the effect of this? (2 marks)

❸ After reading the whole passage, what impressions do you get about the writer's relationship with the villagers? Write your answer on a separate sheet.

Write about:

■ the way she describes their behaviour
■ the use of language and imagery
■ your personal response to the text. (6 marks)

Reading media texts

Media texts are mostly intended to persuade. They aim to persuade us:
- to buy something
- to do something
- to change our opinion about something.

In the case of newspapers they also aim to inform us and perhaps entertain us.

Some media texts you might expect to study during Key Stage 3 are:
- newspaper article
- holiday *brochure*
- information/advice leaflet
- letter from a charity
- *advertisement*
- *web page*

Understanding a media text

To achieve Level 5 you need to:
- be able to locate information and ideas in the text
- be aware of the purpose of the text
- note the importance of **layout** features
- note the use of particular words and phrases.

To move from Level 5 to Levels 6 and 7 you also need to:
- comment on the way layout features have been used
- comment on the way particular **language** devices have been used
- say how successful the writer has been in achieving their purpose
- give a personal response to the text.

Newspaper

Aim: to inform, entertain, change **opinion**.
Layout: headline, columns, short paragraphs, pictures.
Language: should be factual though some articles contain bias and opinion, Standard English, headlines use alliteration, puns, etc.

Web page

Aim: to inform, entertain, persuade, give advice
Layout: pictures, small blocks of text, menu bar / navigation buttons, lots of colour, different font sizes and styles
Language: as a web page can serve the purpose of any of the other media text types, it may draw on any of the language features of the other texts.

Leaflet

Aim: to give information or advice on a particular topic; to **persuade** the reader to change their opinion; to help the reader.

Layout: different font styles and sizes, headings, columns, bullet points, pictures, graphs and charts.

Language: Standard English, fact and opinion, simple sentence structure and vocabulary choices to reach a wider audience.

Advertisement

Aim: to attract attention; to inform; to persuade reader to buy a product or service.

Layout: lots of pictures, different font sizes and styles, bright colours, small blocks of text, slogans and captions.

Language: emotive and persuasive, slogans use alliteration, puns, questions and repetition, more opinion than fact, sometimes use slang expressions.

Charity letter

Aim: to persuade the reader to give money or get involved in a project.

Layout: short paragraphs, standard letter layout, bold type, tear-off sections, pictures.

Language: Standard English, emotive language, fact and opinion.

Holiday brochure

Aim: to persuade the reader to buy a holiday.

Layout: lots of pictures, tables and charts, short blocks of text, different font sizes.

Language: emotive and persuasive, fact and opinion, descriptions in note form often using abbreviations.

KEY TERMS

Make sure you understand these terms before moving on!

- aim
- layout
- language
- advertisement
- brochure
- opinion
- persuade
- web page

Glossary of media terms

Later in this section, you will find some examples of how to comment on the features of media texts. If you simply identify these features, you will achieve Level 4. You must say how and why these features are used to achieve Level 5 or higher.

Newspaper

Broadsheet: a newspaper, considered to be more factual and serious than a **tabloid**. Aims to inform and report, not to entertain. Broadsheets were traditionally the larger of the two newspaper styles, although many have now adopted a smaller format. Examples: **The Guardian** and **The Times**.

Columns: newspaper and magazine articles are set out in columns; leaflets sometimes use this format too. Columns break up a page and make it more interesting to look at.

Headlines: in newspapers they are particularly important attention grabbers. They are made deliberately dramatic so that the audience will read on. In **tabloid** newspapers headlines are often linked to **pictures** to make up the majority of the front page. Language devices such as **alliteration**, **rhyme** and repetition are often used.

Pictures: in newspapers they are used to back up and dramatise or personalise a story – they are often closely linked with **headlines**.

Quotations: a direct comment taken from someone involved in the newspaper story. This gives the report validity and can often give a more personalised feel. Reporters are required to be unbiased and give a balanced account of the story, but the people involved will often be on one side or another.

Short paragraphs: long paragraphs can be off-putting for a busy reader. Most media texts are organised into short paragraphs to hold attention.

Tabloid: this kind of newspaper is considered to be less serious and, sometimes, less factual than a broadsheet. As well as reporting, these papers also aim to entertain. Examples: **The Sun** and **The Mirror**.

Topic sentence: the first sentence of a newspaper story, closely linked to the **headline**. It usually tells you who, what, when and where the story happened.

Other terms

Audience: the readership that a text is aimed at. In advertising, a lot of market research is done so that products can be aimed at very specific groups of people.

Tone of voice: this often indicates the emotions and feelings that the writer wishes to put across to the reader. Examples of tone of voice could be persuasive, conversational, informative, tempting, dramatic or conspiratorial. You would not expect the tone to be aggressive or superior as this would put the reader off.

Leaflet

Bold print: darker print makes important information stand out from the rest of the text.

Bullet points: often marked out with an asterisk or small symbol, these short sentences or phrases attract the attention of the busy reader.

Font styles: different styles of printing are used to make text look different or attractive. Sometimes a particular font may be used to link it to the subject of the text.

Frames and borders: sections of text may be boxed in to highlight their importance or to group together text that covers the same topic.

Graphs and charts: used to demonstrate the facts in a clear visual way; they can be used to back up claims made in the text and can be quite dramatic.

Pictures: in leaflets they can be emotive, e.g. a picture of a lonely pensioner or a starving African child.

Subheadings: are like signposts to the important information in any text. Key words and phrases are picked out to focus the reader's attention.

SOME EXAMPLES OF THE DIFFERENT STYLES USED FOR MAKING LEAFLETS

EXAMPLES OF DIFFERENT styles used for creating a leaflet.

Examples of different styles used for creating a leaflet. Examples of different styles.

used for creating a leaflet. Examples of different styles used for creating a leaflet

Advertisement

Personal pronouns: in persuasive writing, particularly advertising, the pronouns **you** and **we** are used extensively. This is to make the reader feel that they are being addressed individually and personally. This also works in charity appeals. E.g. **You** could make a difference if **you** give just £5.

Pictures: in advertising, pictures can be more important than the text. They can be tempting and colourful or more stylised, perhaps black and white.

Slogans: main use is in advertising. They are 'catchphrases' linked to the product, aimed to stick in the minds of the target audience. Slogans make use of language devices such as: **alliteration**, e.g. The Totally Tropical Taste; **repetition**, e.g. Have a break. Have a Kit Kat; **puns**, e.g. Bakers born and bread, and **questions**, e.g. Have you had your Weetabix?

Text size: important information is in larger print; less appealing information – terms and conditions, for example – tend to be smaller.

WE CLEAN 'EM

OH BOY! IT LOOKS NEW!

Have a go...

Try to identify some of these features in media texts you find at home and in school.

Example text

Study this leaflet carefully. It was produced to encourage healthy eating. Look closely at the annotated sections and see if you can work out how each of these details would back up your answers to the four basic questions at the foot of the page.

Headings: break up the text and draw your attention to important information.

Columns: break up the text and make it easier to scan.

Text: empathises with parents of young children.

Bullet points: show the important information in quick note form.

It's never too early to introduce healthy habits

Healthy Eating can be Fun!

Of course you want what's best for your child but sometimes getting the balance right can be hard. All parents dread turning meal times into a battleground and it can be tempting to swap healthy fruit for a bowl of tempting ice cream. But healthy choices can also be fun. Follow this simple advice to avoid problems and keep mealtimes happy.

Fast Food Fun!

Fast food doesn't need to mean junk food. Fruit and vegetables make the ideal snacks: after school; after sports; on the move or for a TV treat:

- Bananas are the ultimate fast food, no preparation needed, just unzip and enjoy
- Dried apricots and raisins make a great alternative to sweets or chocolate
- Ready chopped sticks of carrot, cucumber and red or yellow pepper are delicious to crunch on with a favourite dip.
- Keep a bowl of ready washed and chopped fruit on an easy to reach shelf in the fridge and encourage your children to help themselves if they feel a bit peckish.

I hate sprouts!

Some vegetables do a have a strong taste which children may dislike. You could try disguising some of these stronger flavours by mixing with cheese sauce or tomato sauce. Many vegetables have naturally sweet flavours which will appeal to young children. Delicious puddings are easy to create with some added fruity goodness.

- Make your own tomato sauce. Onions, carrots, celery and peppers could be whizzed up with tinned tomatoes to make a delicious and versatile sauce. Try it as a pizza base, with pasta shapes or in your own Bolognese sauce.

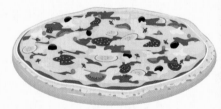

- Broccoli or cauliflower cheese is a meal in itself or a tasty side dish.

The text is explained on pages 42-43.

Five-a-Day – The Easy Way!

- Add carrot or sweet potato to ordinary mashed potato
- Mix pureed fruit with Greek yoghurt or fromage frais
- Use fresh or tinned fruit in jellies

What counts in our Five-a-Day?

- Fresh fruit and vegetables
- Frozen vegetables
- Dried fruit
- Fresh fruit juice
- Tinned fruit and vegetables

Get stuck in!

Encourage your child to help you in the kitchen. They will be keen to eat it if they've helped to make it!

- Try making pizza together with that yummy tomato sauce
- Cheesy courgette muffins are hard to beat but simple to bake
- What about having your own take away night and making a quick and easy stir fry with lots of brightly coloured vegetables

Or what about growing your own fruit and vegetables? Even the smallest garden, yard or window box has room for a tomato plant or a pot of baby carrots.

Imperative verbs: are used for instructions.

Pictures: make the fruit and vegetables look colourful, tasty and convenient to eat.

Why is the Five-a-Day rule important?

Fruit and vegetables are full of vitamins, minerals and fibre – all essential for good health, especially when it comes to fighting off germs picked up at nursery or in the school playground. Experts are all in agreement that eating the recommended five portions of fruit or vegetables can lower the risk of serious health problems in later life including heart disease, cancer, stroke and type 2 diabetes. So if you want to give your child the best start in life, get started and go for five now!

If you would like more information about growing your own fruit and vegetables or quick and easy recipes for healthy meals and snacks, please complete the order form overleaf.

 Questions you should consider: Who is it aimed at? Why has it been written? What is the main idea or message? How is that message put across?

The text explained

The main purpose of this leaflet is to give advice to parents about how to get their children to eat more fruit and vegetables. However, it uses many persuasive techniques to make parents feel it's worth making the effort to encourage their children to adopt a healthy diet.

The text explained

Who? The leaflet is aimed at parents of young children who may be concerned about what they eat and how to provide a more healthy diet.

What? The main idea is that healthy eating can be made fun for children and it doesn't have to be time consuming for busy parents.

Why? It has been written to encourage parents to introduce more fruit and vegetables to their children's diets and to promote good health habits.

How? The text is full of straightforward advice about what your child should eat and how to make this fun and easy. The presentation is simple and attractive.

Content

- There is a balance of fact and opinion, allowing the writer to give factual information but to be persuasive at the same time: 'Fruit and vegetables are full of vitamins, minerals and fibre'; 'They will be keen to eat it if they've helped to make it!'
- Experts are mentioned to make people believe that the advice is medically sound.
- There are lots of suggestions to make fruit and vegetables more appealing to children.

Make sure you can spot the difference between fact and opinion. Watch out for opinions being presented as facts. Non-fiction and media texts often use opinion to manipulate the reader.

Language

- The language is straightforward and easy to understand. This is because it is aimed at all parents of young children rather than a specialist group. The language in a healthy-eating leaflet for medical professionals would probably contain lots of specialist medical vocabulary.
- It is written in Standard English so that everyone can understand it and important information isn't misunderstood.
- The tone of voice is informal – conversational and friendly. Although it is telling people to change their children's eating habits, it doesn't come across as being overly instructive in tone.
- There are suggestions rather than orders: "What about having your own take away night…" Some sections include **imperatives** because they are giving serving or preparation instructions in the same way a recipe would use the imperative: "Make your own..", "Add carrot or sweet potato…", "Mix pureed fruit…"
- Questions are used to introduce new sections to give the idea that the leaflet responds to common parental concerns: "Why is the five-a-day rule important?"

Layout

A variety of layout features are used in this leaflet.

Pictures: the front cover is a full-page picture of a child eating a water melon. She looks healthy and happy. Inside there are a number of colourful pictures which break up the text and back up the message that fruit and vegetables can be tasty and fun.

Headings: each of the main sections has a heading to attract attention and break up the text.

Bullet points: suggestions for serving are broken up with bullet points making it quick and easy to read.

Columns: these are used to break up the text into manageable chunks; the columns are themselves broken up with pictures.

 When writing about layout features you must explain how they make the whole text more effective.

 KEY TERMS

Make sure you understand these terms before moving on!
- imperative
- layout
- bullet point
- picture
- heading

Media test

Use the questions to test your progress. Check your answers on page 94.

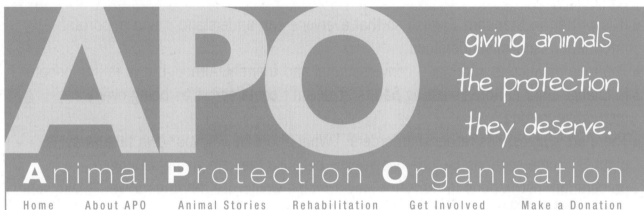

APO
giving animals the protection they deserve.

Animal **P**rotection **O**rganisation

| Home | About APO | Animal Stories | Rehabilitation | Get Involved | Make a Donation |

Animal Stories

Mog's Tale

Alfie's Story

A Dog's Life

Rehabilitation

How you can help

Find your nearest APO centre

◀ up to 10 miles

◀ your postcode

search

Results...

Sign up for our email information service

Register

Donate online now

Mog's Tale

Just months ago, this beautiful little kitten was unrecognisable after being subjected to terrifying cruelty.

She had been wrapped in sellotape and the tip of her tail had been badly damaged – probably repeatedly stamped on.

She was brought to one of our rescue centres where trained volunteers work alongside vets to care for animals injured or neglected by careless owners.

Thanks to their round the clock care and attention, Mog has made a good recovery. Her fur has re-grown and although the tip of her tail has been amputated she is able to jump and balance without any problems.

Mog has now been found a safe and loving home. She is learning to enjoy life as a proper family pet.

Not so lucky

Believe it or not, Mog is one of the lucky ones! Every year hundreds of animals are brought to our centres around the country and even our expert care cannot save them. That's why we need your help and generous donations to continue our fight to prevent this mindless cruelty happening in the first place.

We need your help!

Whether it is your time volunteering, your generous donations of money or your support for our campaign work, we cannot continue to be successful without you. Kittens like Mog need your help and just a small regular gift of £2 a month could make all the difference in a life or death situation.

__Click here to make a donation now.__

 Read the text. Annotate the text. Answer the questions.

Who is it aimed at?

....

....

....

....

....

....

What is the main idea/message in the text?

....

....

....

....

....

Why has it been written?

....

....

....

....

....

How is that message put across?

....

....

....

....

....

PRACTICE QUESTIONS

❶ Find and copy an example of a fact and an opinion used in this text and explain how each is effective.

Fact:

Explanation:

Opinion:

Explanation: (4 marks)

❷ In the sections 'Not So Lucky' and 'We Need Your Help!', which personal pronouns are most often used and what effect does this have?

Personal pronouns:

Explanation: (2 marks)

❸ Write about the way in which language, layout and presentational devices have been used to persuade the reader to donate via the APO website. Write your answer on a separate sheet.

Write about:

- the use of pictures
- font size and style
- general organisation
- specific words and phrases. (6 marks)

Writing to entertain

Imaginative writing

To achieve Level 5 you need to:
- experiment with **figurative language**
- create **believable characters**
- use **language** and **structure** to create atmosphere
- organise writing into paragraphs and make clear links between them.

To move from Level 5 to Levels 6 and 7 you also need to:
- maintain a balance of **plot, description** and **dialogue**
- vary the pace by using a **range of sentence structures**
- control and sequence your writing
- **sustain** and **develop characters** and **settings** in narrative
- experiment with and control a **range of narrative styles**
- shape and craft paragraphs for imaginative effect.

Features of imaginative writing

Creating a good piece of **imaginative** writing is similar to following a recipe. There are some basic ingredients that you need to include. They are:
- plot/story-line
- characterisation
- relationships
- setting
- **descriptive** language
- **dialogue**.

These are the same elements that were discussed in **Reading Fiction**. Go back to that chapter for more information.

> *In the long writing task you will be awarded marks for: sentence structure and punctuation, text structure and organisation and composition and effect.*

Before you begin – imaginative writing

Before you begin to write you will need to plan and make some decisions.

Decide:
- what kind of story you want to write
- a basic plot outline
- third- or first-person **narrative**
- who your main characters are
- where the story is set.

Plan:
- the content of the beginning, middle and end of your story (see Structure pages 50–51)
- character detail
- some descriptive detail.

 In the National Curriculum, writing at Level 5 is described as: 'varied and interesting ... vocabulary choices are imaginative'.

Making your writing more interesting – extending vocabulary

- In order to achieve Level 5 you have to make use of interesting words and phrases. Think about how you can extend your vocabulary by replacing everyday words with something a little more imaginative.
- Instead of 'nice' how about:

great   amazing   breath-taking   beautiful   attractive

superb   lovely   fine   excellent   magnificent

That's really nice...

Some words are more powerful than others. Your choice of vocabulary should also take account of how strong a word is. What order would you put these words and phrases in?

really nice	warm
absolutely fantastic	hot
quite good	scorched
satisfactory	boiling
appalling	tepid
very entertaining	balmy
reasonably satisfied	fiery

Have a go...

Think of five alternatives for each of the following words. Try to put them in order according to how powerful each word is.

scared	excited
run	fall
angry	cold

 KEY TERMS

Make sure you understand these terms before moving on!
- narrative
- dialogue
- descriptive
- vocabulary
- imaginative

Characters & atmosphere

To keep your writing interesting, you need to think beyond an exciting story-line. You must also create believable *characters* and the right *atmosphere*.

Creating atmosphere

The main elements used to create atmosphere are:

- the setting
- the way a character behaves
- use of **language devices**
- sentence **structure**
- vocabulary choices.

If you wanted to create a frightening atmosphere, you might include some of the following ideas.

Setting: city at night, forest, beach during winter, castle or unoccupied building.

Character behaviour: nervous, jumpy.

Language devices: e.g. 'shadows danced like demented spirits'.

Sentence structure: short sentences and repetition.

Vocabulary: e.g. isolated, deserted, gloomy, dank, murky.

Believable characters

If the characters in your stories are to be convincing you need to know them before you start writing. Making a character fact file is an effective way to do this.

Have a go now...

Name:	Leisure/hobbies:
Age:	Ambition:
Occupation:	Fears:
Appearance:	Family:
Personality:	Past/secret:

Convincing dialogue

Dialogue is another word for speech or conversation. Most fiction contains dialogue because it allows the main characters to communicate with each other. Dialogue is important for the following reasons:

- it helps to bring the characters to life
- it reveals new information about the character speaking or the character being spoken about
- it adds variety to the story.

It is important to think about how characters say things as well as what they say.

Re-read this conversation from *A Kestrel for a Knave*. You read a longer extract in the **Fiction test** (pages 16–17). Think about what we learn about the characters from this dialogue.

The exclamation marks show that Billy is in pain or discomfort.

Notice that the conversation is written as these people would really speak. 'Gi'o'er' is how Billy would say 'Give over'. Billy doesn't speak in Standard English – this style of writing indicates Billy's dialect and accent.

Mr Sugden's final comment shows that he thinks Billy is a liar.

'Got a sweat on Casper?'
'Let me out, Sir. Let me come.'
'I thought you'd like a cooler after your exertions in goal.'
'I'm frozen!'
'Really?'
'Gi'o'er, Sir! It's not right!'
'And was it right when you let that last goal in?'
'I couldn't help it!'
'Rubbish, lad.'

The conversation isn't always written in complete sentences because we don't always speak in complete sentences.

The whole conversation shows that Mr Sugden is more powerful than Billy.

I said, he said, she said…

- Notice that the example above doesn't use any speech descriptors (verbs), e.g. he said, Billy shouted.
- When you use dialogue in a story think about all the different ways there are to describe how somebody says something. Using a variety of speech descriptors gives the reader more information about what a character is like.
- Here are some words you could use to replace 'said':

replied	gasped	shrieked	asked	giggled
squeaked	laughed	screamed	exclaimed	snapped
stammered	urged	answered	shouted	whispered

Have a go…

Decide on a speech descriptor for each line in the conversation above. Choose from the list or use your own ideas.

KEY TERMS

Make sure you understand these terms before moving on!
- atmosphere
- character
- dialect
- language device
- structure
- dialogue

Language & structure

Effective use of language and control of the structure of your writing will help you to achieve Level 5 and above.

Using language

Adjectives and adverbs

Make use of descriptive words to make your writing interesting. For example, He sat down at the table. (simple sentence) Wearily, he sat down at the old, worn table.

adverb   *noun phrase using adjectives*

Colours

Using colour in your descriptions can make them more interesting, especially if you try to be more adventurous than using yellow, red, blue, etc. Here is a list of colours used by Susan Hill in the extract you read earlier: 'ragged black wings'; 'butter-coloured cornstalks'; 'its mouth was scarlet'; 'the tip of its black wing'.

Imagery

Use similes, metaphors and personification in your writing.

Senses

Include images or descriptions that will appeal to the five senses. For example, 'wiping the damp mess of tears and sweat off his face with one hand'. (*I'm the King of the Castle* by Susan Hill.)

Sentence structure

- Try to vary the length and construction of your sentences. This will make your writing more interesting. It will also allow you to use sentence structure for effect. If you have been writing fairly complex sentences, then a sudden change to short, simple sentences could show sudden fear.
- Here is another extract from Susan Hill's writing: 'Sweat was running down his forehead and into his eyes. He looked up. The crow kept on coming. He ran.'
- She could have written: 'He looked up and saw that the crow kept on coming so he ran.' All the dramatic tension is lost in this version.

Time spent planning is time well spent in classroom tasks, homework and tests. In examinations you will sometimes be given specific time for planning your writing. Think about what you are going to write and how you are going to sustain your narrative.

Structure

Your writing needs clearly defined structure. This will usually take the form of three definite stages: the beginning, the middle and the ending.

The beginning

- In the opening section of a piece of imaginative writing, you need to introduce the characters and the setting, and begin to develop the main plot strands.
- It is important to create an interesting opening, as you need to capture the attention of your reader.
- Do not give your reader too much detail. Keep them guessing so that they will want to read on. Never launch straight into 'telling a story'.
- Begin with an interesting description of a character or the setting.
- If you are writing in first-person narrative, you could begin with an intriguing statement from your main character.

The middle

- In the central section of your writing you need to develop plot, characterisation and relationships. Development is essential if you are to hold the interest of the reader.
- If you made a character fact file as preparation, make sure you introduce some details from it. Refer back to your character plans to make sure they react to events in the way their personality suggests.

- Think about how you can use language and structure to make your writing interesting and lively.

The ending

In the final section of your writing, you must begin to tie up loose ends. You have three main options for finishing your writing:

- Cliffhanger: the story ends without **conclusion** or **resolution**. This keeps the reader guessing as to what will happen next. However, you need to leave some clues and have some ideas yourself for what will happen next. You should plan to finish in this way rather than realising you have run out of time. An unfinished ending and a cliffhanger ending are two completely different things!
- Twist in the tale: a completely unexpected twist in the plot right at the end. This is an exciting way to end a story but it is also more difficult to manage. Again, it is important to plan for this kind of ending.
- Resolution: all the loose ends are tied up and the ending is complete and definite. This would often be a happy ending but it doesn't have to be.

Try to avoid **clichéd** endings. You could really ruin a good story for want of an original conclusion. For example, avoid: 'Then I woke up. It had all been a dream!'

Have a go...

Plan the structure for a story about a journey to a new and unfamiliar place.
- Write the opening sentence.
- Decide on which kind of ending you will use.
- Write five main bullet points for each section.
- Think about: characters, setting, plot developments, relationship developments and language.

KEY TERMS

Make sure you understand these terms before moving on!
- sentence structure
- adjective
- adverb
- imagery
- senses
- resolution
- cliché
- conclusion

Writing to inform

Throughout Key Stage 3 you may be required to write in the following styles.
Writing to:
- *inform*, *explain*, describe
- persuade, argue, advise
- review, analyse, comment.

You may have to write in one or more of the following forms:
letter, speech, leaflet, newspaper or magazine article, essay, review.

Good non-fiction

To produce a good piece of non-fiction writing you need to have a clear sense of **purpose**. You need to know what you are trying to achieve as an end result. Usually it will be one of the following:
- communicate information or ideas
- persuade people to buy something, take part in something or change their opinion about something
- express your own opinion.

In every situation you will be targeting a specific **audience**. You need to keep that at the front of your mind when you write. Hopefully, this will help you to keep your writing direct and focused.

Targets for Levels 5–7

To achieve Level 5 you need to:
- make your **meaning clear** in a range of forms
- use a more **formal style** where appropriate
- make **adventurous vocabulary** choices
- organise your writing into paragraphs and make clear links between them.

To move from Level 5 to Levels 6 and 7 you also need to:
- use an **impersonal style** where appropriate
- use a **range of sentence structures** to create effects
- control and sequence your writing
- consistently **match your writing style to the purpose** and **audience** of your writing
- use **paragraphing** and **punctuation** to make the sequence of ideas coherent to the reader

Basic questions

In the **Reading non-fiction** and **Reading media texts** sections of this book, you were advised to ask yourself four basic questions after reading a text. When you write a non-fiction piece, you should be able to apply those same questions to your own work. If the answers are clear then you have done a good job. Those questions are:

Who is it aimed at?

Why has it been written?

What is the main idea/message in the text?

How is that message put across?

Writing to inform

Conventions of information text:

- uses sub-headings
- uses third person
- examples, diagrams and illustrations back up the information in the text
- text is written in the present tense
- the length of sentences is decided by the need for clarity – mostly simple and compound sentences.

Visual variety

Remember that a successful information text needs to hold the reader's attention. Think about the ways you can improve the visual impact of your information text with:

- bullet points
- headings
- colour
- paragraph length.
- pictures
- different font sizes and styles
- tables, charts and graphs

Planning

Decide on the categories of information you are going to provide.

Writing

Your writing style needs to be clear, factual and formal. As you are required to write in the third person, you should use terms such as: Students study a wide range of subjects. Don't use we or I: At school we study lots of different subjects.

Writing to explain

You may be asked to explain:

How?   A decision   Why?   A point of view   A process

Conventions of explanation:

- the opening contains a general statement to introduce the topic
- the development of the explanation draws attention to how something works or why something happens
- there is a summary of what has been explained
- the text is written in the present tense
- the text uses the **passive voice** and technical vocabulary, which gives the piece quite a formal style
- the text uses connectives that indicate cause and effect
- the text uses connectives that indicate sequence.

Use the following connectives in your own writing.

Cause and effect			Sequence	
because	*so*	*due to*	*then*	*next*
therefore	*as a result of*		*finally*	*gradually*

💡 ***Explanation sometimes contains elements of other non-fiction styles: information and persuasion.***

KEY TERMS

Make sure you understand these terms before moving on!

- audience
- purpose
- inform
- explain
- passive voice

Writing to describe

You could be asked to write a *description* of:

■ a person

■ a place

■ or a particular memory.

You will also use writing to describe techniques in writing to imagine, explore and entertain.

It is often a good idea to note down *adjectives*, *images* and particular *details* you want to include in your writing before you decide on the structure of your writing.

Describing people

If you are asked to describe a person in detail, you need to think about lots of different aspects of that person, not just what they look like.

A person I remember clearly from my childhood is my next-door neighbour, Elsie. She was the oldest person I knew. Her skin was like crinkly brown paper and her eyes watered when she laughed. She had delicate, mottled hands and her wedding ring was loose on her finger.

She was generous and kind. Whenever we visited we had jelly sweets or jaffa cakes. She called me 'wench' or 'ducks'. She always seemed to be washing sheets and took great pride in always being first out to hang her washing on the line.

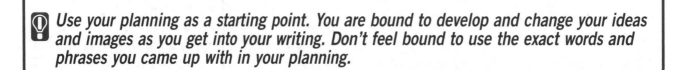 *Use your planning as a starting point. You are bound to develop and change your ideas and images as you get into your writing. Don't feel bound to use the exact words and phrases you came up with in your planning.*

Describing memories

The spider diagram below is planning to answer the following question:

Describe a journey you remember well.

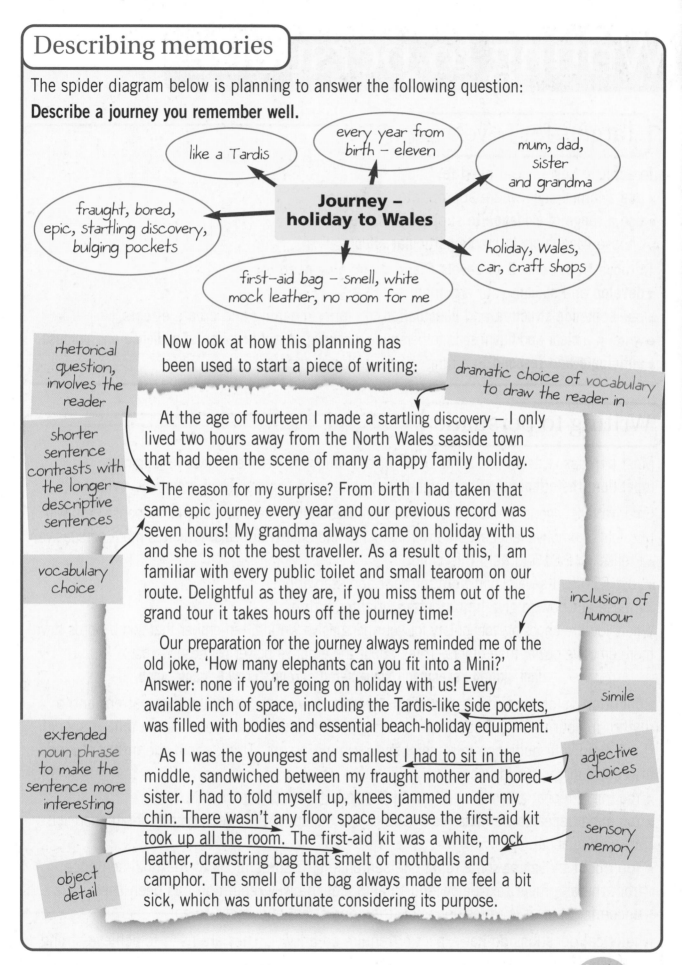

- like a Tardis
- every year from birth – eleven
- mum, dad, sister and grandma
- fraught, bored, epic, startling discovery, bulging pockets
- **Journey – holiday to Wales**
- holiday, Wales, car, craft shops
- first-aid bag – smell, white mock leather, no room for me

Now look at how this planning has been used to start a piece of writing:

dramatic choice of vocabulary to draw the reader in

At the age of fourteen I made a startling discovery – I only lived two hours away from the North Wales seaside town that had been the scene of many a happy family holiday.

rhetorical question, involves the reader

shorter sentence contrasts with the longer descriptive sentences

vocabulary choice

The reason for my surprise? From birth I had taken that same epic journey every year and our previous record was seven hours! My grandma always came on holiday with us and she is not the best traveller. As a result of this, I am familiar with every public toilet and small tearoom on our route. Delightful as they are, if you miss them out of the grand tour it takes hours off the journey time!

inclusion of humour

Our preparation for the journey always reminded me of the old joke, 'How many elephants can you fit into a Mini?' Answer: none if you're going on holiday with us! Every available inch of space, including the Tardis-like side pockets, was filled with bodies and essential beach-holiday equipment.

simile

extended noun phrase to make the sentence more interesting

As I was the youngest and smallest I had to sit in the middle, sandwiched between my fraught mother and bored sister. I had to fold myself up, knees jammed under my chin. There wasn't any floor space because the first-aid kit took up all the room. The first-aid kit was a white, mock leather, drawstring bag that smelt of mothballs and camphor. The smell of the bag always made me feel a bit sick, which was unfortunate considering its purpose.

adjective choices

sensory memory

object detail

KEY TERMS

Make sure you understand these terms before moving on!
- detail
- description
- adjective
- image
- noun phrase
- vocabulary

Writing to persuade

Writing to persuade

Most persuasive texts use some or all of the following devices: emotive language, repetition, rhetorical questions, presenting opinion as fact, counter-argument, evidence.

Emotive language is the use of words and phrases that evoke an emotional response. You will find lots of emotive language in advertisements and charity appeals. Which is more persuasive?
- Please give £10 to help this child.
- Just £10 will save David from torment and starvation.
  Please act now to give him a better, brighter future.

When you are choosing vocabulary for your persuasive writing, remember that some words have more emotive power then others. Think about the emotive power of these words:

died   killed   executed   slaughtered   group   crowd   gang   mob

Repetition helps to reinforce the main points of your text and build up a pattern and a rhythm in your writing. Repetition is particularly useful if you are writing a talk or speech. It will help your audience to remember your main points. Think about the different kinds of repetition you could use.
- You might repeat an emotive phrase at the end of each paragraph.
- You might repeatedly emphasise a good or bad feature of an object, person or situation you are writing about.
- You might try to use some repetitive sentence structures. Look at the final sentence from the argument text below and think about the way repetition has been used: It is uncomfortable; it is unfashionable; it is impractical and it has to go!

Rhetorical questions do not expect or require an answer. They are used to achieve strong emphasis. The writer assumes that the answer to the question is obvious. The question 'How old are you?' clearly requires an answer, whereas 'Makes you think, doesn't it?' is rhetorical and assumes that the answer will be yes.

Argument

Argument is a form of persuasion. If you have a verbal argument with somebody, it is because you disagree with their opinion. To win an argument you must persuade your opponent that your point of view is correct.

A one-sided essay expresses your own opinions about an issue. You may also be asked to write a one-sided argument in the form of a letter or speech. It should be structured as follows:

1 Introduction explaining the issue and giving your opinion.
2 A series of paragraphs to express the main points of your argument. You should include evidence to support your ideas. It is essential that you have a clear argument running through your essay. You should organise your points so that each one builds on the one before. Make sure you order your points to have the most impact.
3 Conclusion summing up your main points and restating your opinion.

Discursive essay

A **discursive** or balanced essay considers two sides of an issue or argument. It should be structured as follows:

1 Introduction explaining the issue
2 An organised series of paragraphs with points in favour of the issue
3 An organised series of paragraphs with points against the issue
4 Conclusion summing up the points for and against and giving your own opinion.

Linking points in your argument

Use the following connectives to link your ideas in persuasion and argument texts:
furthermore   on the other hand   despite the fact that   however   nevertheless
not only   of course   in my opinion

 Discursive argument and advice sometimes use rhetorical questions to introduce new topics or ideas.

Writing to advise

Lots of advice texts contain the **modal verbs** should, would and could.
Look at these examples from advice for looking after a new pet.
■ You should take your dog for a walk at least once a day.
■ You could try basic obedience training once your puppy is old enough.
■ I would suggest a regular check-up with the vet.
Other conventions of advice:
■ uses the imperative
■ makes suggestions
■ sentences tend to be simpler to get information across
■ text is written in the second person
■ can use anecdote/examples
■ sometimes uses rhetorical questions to introduce ideas.

KEY TERMS

Make sure you understand these terms before moving on!
■ emotive language
■ rhetorical question
■ argument
■ modal verb
■ repetition
■ evidence
■ discursive

Writing to review

Writing to review

When you write a **review** of something, you are giving your own opinion. This could be completely different from somebody else's opinion on the same topic. You might be asked to write a review about:

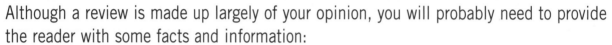

- a book
- a film
- a television programme
- an exhibition.

What to include

Although a review is made up largely of your opinion, you will probably need to provide the reader with some facts and information:

- the title and author/director etc.
- a summary of the story
- information about the exhibition
- where you can buy the book or see the film/exhibition.

The audience of a written review will usually be people who want to know if they would enjoy the book, film or exhibition. You should include your opinions on:

- its strengths
- its weaknesses
- its suitability for a particular audience.

Writing to analyse and comment

Writing to **analyse** and **comment** is probably the most **formal** style of writing you will be required to use in your exams.

Writing style

- Text is written in the third person.
- Opinions are expressed in a detached way – avoid phrases such as 'I think that...'.
- Opinions are supported by textual evidence.
- Avoid non-standard forms and colloquial expression.

💡 *Use Standard English when you write to analyse or comment.*

Structure

An analytical essay should follow a set pattern.
- The **introduction** should refer to key words in the question, capture the attention of the reader and demonstrate an understanding of the question.
- A series of paragraphs should explore different aspects of the question. Paragraphs should be linked and main points should be supported with quotations.
- The **conclusion** should refer back to the main points of your analysis and give your personal response to the question.

Paragraph structure

A useful way to **structure** your analysis in each paragraph is to:
- make a statement or comment
- use quotation or textual evidence to back up your statement
- explain your comment with reference to the evidence you have cited.

This is often referred to as the PEE structure – Point, Evidence, Explanation or PEC – Point, Evidence, Comment.

Some useful phrases...

Use these phrases to help you comment on the effects created by literature and non-fiction texts:

this suggests that...
the author conveys a sense of ... by ...
this is effective because...
this evokes a feeling of...
he creates tension by...
the writer aims to persuade...

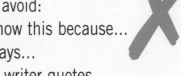

Try to avoid:
I know this because...
it says...
the writer quotes...
this quotation shows that...

 When you are writing to review, keep your audience in mind. Make sure your language is suitable for the audience you have been asked to write for.

KEY TERMS

Make sure you understand these terms before moving on!
- review
- analyse
- comment
- introduction
- conclusion
- structure
- formal

Writing media texts

The main *media* text types you could be asked to write are:

- leaflets
- advertisements
- magazine/newspaper articles.

A good way to learn how to write in this style is to study examples of the style. Re-read the media sections of this book. The glossary on pages 38–39 explains the technical terms.

Leaflets

- Leaflets are usually free and are often handed out or posted through your door at home. For this reason it is important to make an immediate **visual impact** through the use of pictures or bold, eye-catching headings.
- Information, advice or **opinion** needs to be presented in a clear and concise way.
- Information in leaflets needs to appear to be directed at the individual reader. For this reason you should use **personal pronouns**.

Layout and Presentation

The main devices you would use in a leaflet are:

- bullet points
- columns
- pictures.
- short paragraphs
- headings

Have a go...

Write five bullet points about the disadvantages of smoking, aimed at teenagers.

1. ....
2. ....
3. ....
4. ....
5. ....

Think of two presentational devices you might use in a leaflet to persuade teenagers to give up smoking.

1. ....
2. ....

Think of two pictures you could use in the same leaflet.

1. ....
2. ....

> **If you want to include pictures in a leaflet simply draw a box and write what the picture would be.**

Advertisements

As advertising relies so heavily on pictures, it is unlikely that you would be required to write an advertisement in a test.

Some leaflets have an advertising function as well as offering advice or information. Advertising language is very persuasive. If you were asked to design an advert you should think about the following:

- emotive and persuasive language
- devices such as alliteration, repetition, puns and questions
- how to present opinions in a factual way.

Layout and presentation

The main devices you would use are:

- pictures
- different font styles and sizes.

Have a go...

- Think of a new product name and slogan for a box of chocolates.
- Write appealing descriptions of the following chocolates from your new range:

Strawberry cream, Caramel, Dark chocolate and hazelnut, Orange fondant

....

....

....

....

....

....

....

Magazines/newspapers

- News articles report something that has already happened so you must always write in the **past tense**.
- News articles usually report the most dramatic part of an event first and then retell the rest of the story in chronological order.
- News articles are written in Standard English. The only exception to this is direct quotation, which will be written exactly as the person said it.

Layout and presentation

The main devices you would use are:

- pictures
- columns
- short paragraphs
- headlines.

Have a go...

- Write a headline and topic sentence about a lottery winner for a local newspaper.
- Think of two people you would interview for your article.
- Think of a photograph you would want for the story and write a caption to go with it.

....

....

....

KEY TERMS

Make sure you understand these terms before moving on!

- media
- layout
- opinion
- visual impact
- personal pronoun
- past tense

Letters, essays & speeches

Standard English

Formal letters, essays and speeches all require a formal style and Standard English. The following non-standard forms should be avoided.

Using adjectives as adverbs
She won easy. ✗
She won easily. ✔

Mixing singular and plural in subject/verb agreement
He were frightened. ✗
He was frightened. ✔
We was bad. ✗
We were bad. ✔

Using 'them' as a determiner
I bought them oranges. ✗
I bought those oranges. ✔

Using 'what' as a relative pronoun
Have you seen the book what I bought? ✗
Have you seen the book that I bought? ✔

Letter writing dos and don'ts

On many occasions when you write a formal letter, you will be writing to somebody that you have never met before. Remember the following points:
- do use Standard English
- don't use slang or conversational language
- try not to be either aggressive or over-familiar in your tone
- get to your point quickly and stick to your point
- plan the content, structure and accuracy of your letter
- think about the topics that you want to cover and decide on the best order to write about them so your letter flows.

Writing essays

During Key Stage 3 you may be required to write a persuasive essay, a discursive essay or a literary criticism essay that offers analysis and comment on a text you have studied – this could be the Shakespeare play you have studied.

All essays follow these conventions:
- uses formal language/Standard English
- usually written in the third person
- uses evidence, quotation and/or textual reference to support opinion
- follows a structure – introduction, series of linked paragraphs developing a line of argument, conclusion

You will find further information about writing essays on pages 56–59.

Writing a formal letter

There are many reasons why you may need to write a formal letter. For example: to apply for a job; to complain to a company; to apply for a membership; to book a service or to request permission.

There are a lot of conventions to follow when you are writing a formal letter; you may find these conventions vary depending on the type of letter.

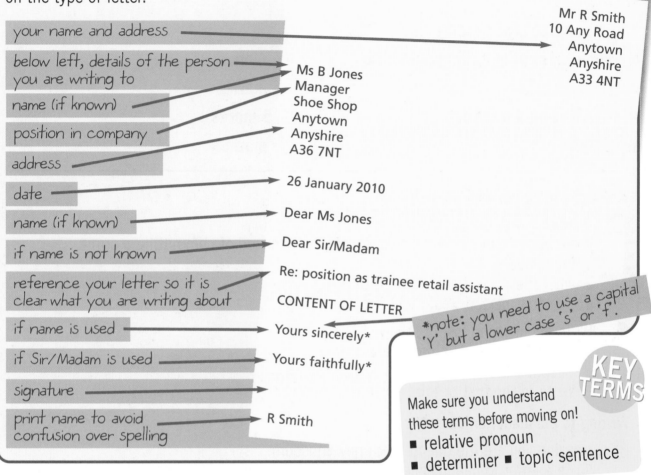

your name and address → Mr R Smith
10 Any Road
Anytown
Anyshire
A33 4NT

below left, details of the person you are writing to → Ms B Jones
Manager
Shoe Shop
Anytown
Anyshire
A36 7NT

name (if known)

position in company

address

date → 26 January 2010

name (if known) → Dear Ms Jones

if name is not known → Dear Sir/Madam

reference your letter so it is clear what you are writing about → Re: position as trainee retail assistant

CONTENT OF LETTER

if name is used → Yours sincerely*

if Sir/Madam is used → Yours faithfully*

signature

print name to avoid confusion over spelling → R Smith

*note: you need to use a capital 'Y' but a lower case 's' or 'f'.

KEY TERMS

Make sure you understand these terms before moving on!
- relative pronoun
- determiner
- topic sentence

Writing speeches

The most important thing to remember about a speech is that your intended audience will be listening to rather than reading what you have written.

Remember this at the planning stage and think about how you can help an audience to follow your line of argument or explanation.

Here are some important devices that make a speech effective.

- **Topic sentences** at the beginning of each paragraph will help your audience to understand the key points and to recognise what they should be listening out for.

- Varied sentence structure and length will allow you to control the **pace** and **rhythms** of your speech. This will keep an audience interested.

- **Repetition** will help the listener to remember your key points.

- **Rhetorical devices**, such as rhetorical questions and listing in groups of three, will also focus your listener on key points.

- A **closing statement** that summarises your argument and restates your main point will make sure the listener goes away in no doubt about the opinion you wanted to express.

Writing test

Use these writing tasks to check your progress. The instructions reflect the type of instructions you may be given if you are taking the Optional Tests.

Spend 45 minutes on this writing task. You should spend 10-15 minutes planning your writing.

You will be awarded marks for:

■ sentence structure and punctuation	(5 marks)
■ text structure and organisation	(5 marks)
■ composition and effect	(15 marks)
■ spelling	(5 marks)

Writing to imagine, explore, entertain

1 'It wasn't me!'
Write about someone wrongly suspected or accused of committing a crime.
Think about:
- what they have been accused of
- how that person would feel.

2 Write about being lost or followed in a forest.
- Try to build up an atmosphere of fear.
- Describe the forest.
- Write in the first or third person.

Writing to persuade, argue, advise

3 Imagine you are the director of a new museum.
Write a letter to headteachers of schools in the area persuading them to bring groups of pupils to the museum.
You could write about:
- what the museum has to offer
- why it is of educational value
- how to organise a trip there.

4 Write a discursive essay about keeping animals in zoos and safari parks.
Write about:
- the points for keeping animals in captivity
- the points against keeping animals in captivity
- your own opinion.

5 Write an advice leaflet for teenagers preparing for exams. Think carefully about your presentation and layout.
You should include:
- advice and suggestions for revision
- what to do in the exam
- tips for relaxing.

Spend 30 minutes on this writing task. You should spend 5-10 minutes planning your writing.

You will be awarded marks for:

- vocabulary (4 marks)
- sentence structure, punctuation and text organisation (8 marks)
- composition and effect (8 marks)

Writing to inform, explain, describe

1 Relationships can be changed or broken up by many things, for example: a move away, death or an argument.
Write about a close relationship that comes to an end.
  - Describe the relationship.
  - Explain why the relationship ended.
  - Try to recreate the emotions involved.

2 Describe a place you have enjoyed visiting.
You could write about:
  - why you like it
  - any specific memories of the place
  - why you would recommend other people to visit this place.

Writing to persuade, argue, advise

3 Imagine you have been given a chance to give a talk to your class. Choose an issue you feel strongly about.
Write a short talk trying to persuade other people to support your views.

Remember the four basic questions to ask about a non-fiction text.
Ask yourself:

1 Who is it aimed at?
2 Why has it been written?
3 What is the main idea or message in the text?
4 How is that message put across?

Shakespeare

During Key Stage 3 you will study at least one play by William Shakespeare. If your school uses the Year 9 Optional Tests, there is one exam paper which focuses on your reading and understanding of a Shakespeare play.

Understanding Shakespeare

To achieve Level 5 you need to:
- begin to read beneath the surface for **meaning**
- note the **effect of particular words** and **phrases**
- show some **understanding** of the **feelings and behaviour of the character**s
- show some understanding of **stagecraft**.

To move from Level 5 to Levels 6 and 7 you also need to:
- **support your ideas** about characters and relationships with **detailed reference to the text**
- write in some detail about the writer's **use of language, structure** of the text and **stagecraft**
- comment on the **creation of setting and atmosphere**
- show **understanding** of the more **complex feelings** of the characters
- recognise what the writer is trying to achieve and how they do this
- trace the **development of plot, character and relationships** and **themes**
- give a **personal** and **critical response** to the text.

What you will study

- If you are preparing for the Year 9 Optional Tests there will be two scenes selected for testing in your exam. You will spend more time studying these scenes closely. Your teacher will explain which scenes you will study in detail.
- If your understanding of Shakespeare is being tested through ongoing class work, your study of a play may be more general.
- Your teacher will decide whether you will read the whole play, watch a film version or watch a live performance of the play.
- Even if you are only studying a few scenes from your Shakespeare play, you need to understand how these scenes relate to the rest of the play, so if you can watch a performance of the play it will be really helpful.

KEY TERMS

Make sure you understand these terms before moving on!
- language
- theme
- performance
- stagecraft
- relationship
- character

What you will be tested on

In the Year 9 Optional Tests you will answer one question on the set scenes from the Shakespeare you have studied. The task you complete will be based on one of four areas of assessment:

- text in performance
- language of the text
- character and motivation
- ideas, themes and issues.

If your understanding of Shakespeare is being tested through your ongoing class work or a teacher set assessment, it is likely to cover one or more of these areas.

In the Optional Tests you will probably be required to write in the form of analysis and comment. Your ongoing class work may also include: writing in role; dramatic role play and writing instruction for how scenes from the play should be performed.

Text in performance

In this area of assessment you would need to write about Shakespeare's use of stagecraft. You might consider:

- the order of scenes to create different effects on the audience
- any difficulties in staging a live performance in comparison to film versions.
- the timing of entrances and exits
- the use of soliloquies and asides
- the use of stage directions and action
- the pace and mood of a scene.

Character and motivation

In this area of assessment you would need to write about how Shakespeare develops different characters and what drives them to act as they do.
You might consider:

- how characters change as the play progresses
- how their behaviour reveals their character
- how relationships between characters are developed
- why characters behave in the way they do.

Language of the text

In this area of assessment you would need to analyse the language used by Shakespeare.
You might consider:

- use of imagery
- use of puns or humour
- use of verse or prose
- how language reflects the mood of the characters or creates atmosphere.

Ideas, themes and issues

In this area of assessment you would need to write about how particular themes and ideas are introduced, developed and explored:

- how the action in particular scenes introduces or develops key themes
- how language is used to develop themes
- why Shakespeare may have focused on particular themes
- how the audience might respond to particular themes and ideas.

Understanding Shakespeare's language

Studying Shakespeare can often seem quite daunting. Again, as with poetry, this is simply because it is less familiar and perhaps seems unconnected to modern-day concerns. However, Shakespeare's plays cover the same themes as any modern piece of writing: love, jealousy, ambition, family conflicts, murder and intrigue. Once the barriers of language have been broken down it is easy to see this.

How to read Shakespeare aloud

Shakespeare's language is always much easier to understand when it is read well. Follow these tips:

- Read to the punctuation. If there is no punctuation at the end of a line then read straight through to the next line.
- Don't rush. Speak clearly and think about what you are saying.
- Words ending in 'd or -ed. If a word is spelt 'd, e.g. accus'd, you pronounce it as we would say accused. However, if it is spelt accused in the text you pronounce the -ed as a separate **syllable** – accuse-ed.
- Think about the tone of voice you should use.
- Think about what your character would do when saying the lines.
- Emphasise the words you think are most important. The natural **stresses** of **iambic pentameter** should help you to do this.

Thee … thou … who?

art	are
hadst	had
hence	here
ill	bad
o'er	over
thee	you
thou	you *(used with someone very close to you or as an insult)*
you	you *(a more distant way of speaking to someone)*
thy	your
whence	where
whither	where
wouldst	would

Rhyme and rhythm

Blank verse: unrhymed lines of iambic pentameter. Shakespeare wrote his plays in blank verse because it is versatile, it is not restricted by rhyme and it is the closest to the natural rhythms of speech. This makes it easy to create different moods – anger, love, etc.

Iambic pentameter: describes the number of syllables and stresses in a line, which is known as the meter. A foot is a pair of syllables. An iambic foot is an unstressed syllable followed by a stressed syllable. There are five iambic feet in iambic pentameter.

Richard:

Now **is** / the **win** / ter **of** / our **dis** / cont**ent**

Made **glo** / rious **sum** / mer **by** / this **sun** / of **York**:

(*Richard III* Act 1, Scene 1)

Rhyming couplets: sometimes Shakespeare wrote in different styles for contrast. More formal and traditional characters making important speeches may speak in rhyming couplets (the lines rhyme in pairs). Because of the constraint of finding rhymes there is less movement and freedom in these speeches. This reflects the characters' formality.

Capulet:

At my poor house look to behold this **night**

Earth-treading stars that make heaven **light**

(*Romeo and Juliet Act 1, Scene 2*)

Prose: the 'low characters', servants for example, speak in prose rather than verse. This reflects that they have less education and their subject matter is often low or coarse.

Trinculo:

I shall laugh myself to death at this puppy-headed monster.

A most scurvy monster! I could find in my heart to beat him –

(*The Tempest* Act 2, Scene 2)

KEY TERMS

Make sure you understand these terms before moving on!
- iambic pentameter
- syllable
- stress
- couplet
- prose
- blank verse

Shakespeare's language

This is an extract from Romeo and Juliet (Act 1, scene 1). Romeo is in love with a woman from a family that his family hate. When he arrives on the scene, he finds that the families have been fighting again.

Romeo and Juliet

O me! – What fray was here?
Yet tell me not, for I have heard it all.
Here's much to do with hate, but more with love.
Why then, O brawling love! O loving hate!
O anything, of nothing first create!
O heavy lightness! serious vanity!
Mis-shapen chaos of well-seeming forms!
Feather of lead, bright smoke, cold fire, sick health!

Romeo and Juliet (Act 1, Scene 1, lines 178–185)

Lines 178–9

Romeo is surprised by the violent scene he sees. He asks for an explanation but then realises that it is the same conflict that always happens. We can tell he is unhappy and that he doesn't like the fighting.

Line 180

He mentions love and hate in the same line, this shows he is confused because he loves a woman he should hate.

Line 181

The reversal of **brawling love** and **loving hate**, emphasises Romeo's confusion.

Lines 183–5

The list of **oxymorons** again emphasise Romeo's confusion and conflicting feelings; he is unhappy when he should be happy (in love) and in love when he should hate. All of the contradictions are negative, which shows that he is depressed and unhappy. This is because Rosaline, the woman he loves, will not return his love. The fact that Romeo talks only about his feelings and lists the **oxymorons** in such a dramatic way shows that he is caught up in his own feelings. You might even think that he is almost enjoying torturing himself and wallowing in his misery.

This extract from later on in the play (Act 3, Scene 1) shows Romeo furious and ready to fight. Tybalt has killed his best friend, Mercutio, and Romeo wants revenge.

Romeo and Juliet

Alive! in triumph! and Mercutio slain!
Away to heaven respective lenity,
And fire-ey'd fury be my conduct now! -
Now, Tybalt, take the villain back again,
That late thou gav'st me; for Mercutio's soul
Is but a little way above our heads,
Staying for thine to keep him company:
Either thou, or I, or both, must go with him.

Romeo and Juliet (Act 3, Scene 1, lines 126–133)

Line 126

The exclamation marks show that Romeo is angry. They also mark the three circumstances that fuel his anger. If Mercutio is dead then Tybalt shouldn't be alive or triumphant.

Line 127

As he is now related to Tybalt, it is **proper** that he should **forgive** him anything – this is the meaning of **respective lenity**. He shouts for these proper feelings to go away. He wants to be angry and out of control.

Line 128

Fire-ey'd fury is like the modern day expression "seeing red". Romeo wants to be ruled by his anger and blinded by rage, he does not want to see the consequences of his actions. If he thought about it, he wouldn't be able to continue – he is about to kill his wife's cousin.

Lines 130–3

When he says that Mercutio is waiting (staying) for Tybalt to keep him company, he is reminding himself of why he has to act. He says that either Tybalt or himself or both of them will have to die. This shows that he is prepared to fight to the death for his friend's memory.

Overall tone

The whole tone of this speech is angry. The language used shows Romeo trying to make himself more and more angry so he can put the consequences out of his mind. He mentions heaven but he sends his "proper feelings" there. *Fire-ey'd* fury is more appropriate to hell; perhaps he feels his behaviour will condemn him to hell if he does kill Tybalt. **Remember** that religion and the consequences of sin were very important in Shakespeare's time.

Revision techniques & tasks

The following ideas will help you to organise your thoughts about the play you have studied. Once you have completed these tasks, the best way to revise is to answer practice questions. You will find some example questions in the test section.

Revision techniques and tasks

Make a timeline of important events in the play. Leave space to make notes about key scenes and connections between them. For example:

Much Ado About Nothing

CONNECTIONS	EVENTS
	– Don Pedro and his friends Claudio and Benedick arrive in Messina
	– Beatrice and Benedick renew their war of words
Don John tries to make Claudio jealous later by claiming that Don Pedro woos Hero for himself	– Claudio is in love with Hero, Don Pedro offers to woo Hero on his behalf, Benedick claims he will never fall in love

Make spider diagrams for each of the main characters to trace **plot involvement**, **relationships** and **personality**. For example:

Hated by Oliver for his goodness

Considers himself to be unlucky

Saves his brother

As You Like It: Orlando / Character

Badly treated by Oliver

Insists on fighting the wrestler Charles

In love with Rosalind

sycorax's son and Prospero's slave

vows to serve Stephano instead of Prospero

wants revenge on Prospero for all his cruelty

found by Stephano and Trinculo

The Tempest: Caliban/plot involvement

persuades Stephano to kill Prospero and seize Miranda

asks forgiveness and is set free

tries to carry out the plot but is tricked by Prospero

Key themes

Pick out the key **themes** in your scenes and find **quotations** that link to this theme in other scenes. If you have your own copy of the play, mark the quotations in your text, using a different colour for each theme. If you don't have your own copy then write out the quotations and colour-code them.

Language

Make a close study of the language used by the main characters in your scenes. Think about:
■ how it helps to create an atmosphere
■ how it helps to show the development of relationships
■ what it shows us about the personality or intentions of those characters.

Action in the rest of the play

Make a list or table to show:
■ how the action in your scenes is affected by preceding scenes
■ how the action in your scenes affects the rest of the play.

....
....
....
....
....
....
....
....
....
....
....
....
....

Practice questions

Practise questions from the four possible assessment areas: text in performance; character and motivation; language of the text; ideas, themes and issues.
You will find some example questions later in this section.

KEY TERMS

Make sure you understand these terms before moving on!
■ theme
■ quotation
■ plot involvement
■ relationship
■ personality

Language study

Make a close study of the language in the extracts from three Shakespeare plays.
Try to identify important words and phrases, language devices and imagery.

As You Like It

JAQUES   All the world's a stage,
And all the men and women merely players:
They have their exits and their entrances;
And one man in his time plays many parts,
His acts being seven ages. At first the infant,
Mewling and puking in the nurse's arms.
And then the whining school-boy, with his satchel
And shining morning face, creeping like snail
Unwillingly to school. And then the lover,
Sighing like furnace, with a woeful ballad
Made to his mistress' eyebrow. Then a soldier,
Full of strange oaths and bearded like the pard,
Jealous in honour, sudden and quick in quarrel,
Seeking the bubble reputation
Even in the cannon's mouth. And then the justice,
In fair round belly with good capon lined,
With eyes severe and beard of formal cut,
Full of wise saws and modern instances;
And so he plays his part. The sixth age shifts
Into the lean and slipper'd pantaloon,
With spectacles on nose and pouch on side,
His youthful hose, well saved, a world too wide
For his shrunk shank; and his big manly voice,
Turning again toward childish treble, pipes
And whistles in his sound. Last scene of all,
That ends this strange eventful history,
Is second childishness and mere oblivion,
Sans teeth, sans eyes, sans taste, sans everything.

As You Like It (Act 2, Scene 7, lines 139–166)

Romeo and Juliet

CAPULET   God's bread! it makes me mad:
Day, night, hour, tide, time, work, play,
Alone, in company, still my care hath been

Romeo and Juliet

To have her match'd: and having now provided
A gentleman of noble parentage,
Of fair demesnes, youthful, and nobly train'd,
Stuff'd, as they say, with honourable parts,
Proportion'd as one's thought would wish a man;
And then to have a wretched puling fool,
A whining mammet, in her fortune's tender,
To answer 'I'll not wed; I cannot love,
I am too young; I pray you, pardon me.'
But, as you will not wed, I'll pardon you:
Graze where you will you shall not house with me:
Look to't, think on't, I do not use to jest.
Thursday is near; lay hand on heart, advise:
An you be mine, I'll give you to my friend;
And you be not, hang, beg, starve, die in the streets,
For, by my soul, I'll ne'er acknowledge thee,
Nor what is mine shall never do thee good:
Trust to't, bethink you; I'll not be forsworn.

Romeo and Juliet (Act 3, Scene 5, lines 176-195)

The Tempest

Enter CALIBAN with a burden of wood. A noise of thunder heard

CALIBAN   All the infections that the sun sucks up
From bogs, fens, flats, on Prosper fall and make him
By inch-meal a disease! His spirits hear me
And yet I needs must curse. But they'll nor pinch,
Fright me with urchin-shows, pitch me i' the mire,
Nor lead me, like a firebrand, in the dark
Out of my way, unless he bid 'em; but
For every trifle are they set upon me;
Sometime like apes that mow and chatter at me
And after bite me, then like hedgehogs, which
Lie tumbling in my barefoot way and mount
Their pricks at my footfall; sometime am I
All wound with adders who with cloven tongues
Do hiss me into madness.

Enter TRINCULO

Lo, now, lo!
Here comes a spirit of his, and to torment me
For bringing wood in slowly. I'll fall flat;
Perchance he will not mind me.

The Tempest (Act 2, Scene 2, lines 1–19)

Shakespeare test

- Use the questions below to check your progress. Some general guidance about how levels would be awarded is included on page 95.

- These questions are very general so that they can be applied to different extracts from a range of plays. Choose the questions that are the best fit for your play and the specific extracts you have been studying.

- Remember to support your comments and opinions with relevant quotation and textual evidence.

Text in performance

How would you direct two key scenes from the Shakespeare play you have studied to create an appropriate atmosphere? You should:
- Give direction about how characters should behave
- Give direction about how lines should be spoken
- Give explanation about why a particular atmosphere is required

Why are these scenes important to the play's development as a whole? You should write about:
- What happens before and after these scenes
- How Shakespeare changes or maintains pace and atmosphere with these scenes

Character and motivation

Comment on the behaviour of the main character(s) in two key scenes from the Shakespeare play you have studied. You should write about:
- The language they use
- The way they behave towards other characters
- How their character(s) change or develop between the two scenes

How are relationships developed in two key scenes from the Shakespeare play you have studied? You should write about:
- The language the characters use
- The way characters behave towards each other
- The way events in the play have affected their relationship

Language of the text

How does Shakespeare use language to demonstrate the inner feelings of a character in two key scenes you have studied? You should write about:

- Use of imagery
- The difference between what the character says when alone on stage and what s/he says to others

Compare the language used by high status and low status characters in the scenes you have studied. You should write about:

- Use of imagery
- Use of verse or prose
- Use of humour

Ideas, themes and issues

How does Shakespeare use these scenes to explore an issue that would have concerned his audience? You should write about:

- How this issue is introduced
- How character behaviour might reflect or challenge the audience's opinion about the issue
- How language is used to explore the issue

How do your selected scenes develop the key theme of this play? You should write about:

- What characters say to develop the theme
- How the action in these scenes relates to the theme

Spelling, punctuation & grammar

Spelling

The best ways to improve your **spelling** are:
- learn spelling rules
- learn commonly misspelt words
- practise spelling strategies.

To achieve Level 5 you need to:
- spell basic words and regular **polysyllabic** words (words with more than one syllable) correctly. In other words, you should be able to spell words that follow spelling rules and fit into patterns with other words.

To move from Level 5 to Levels 6 and 7 you also need to:
- spell irregular polysyllabic words (words that do not fit patterns and are more commonly misspelt).

Punctuation

To achieve Level 5 you need to:
- use full stops, capital letters and question marks accurately
- use **commas** to mark clauses
- use **apostrophes** and **speech punctuation** correctly.

To move from Level 5 to Levels 6 and 7 you also need to:
- use **punctuation** to develop a **range of complex sentences**
- use **punctuation** to **clarify meaning and create effects**.

Grammar

To achieve Level 5 you need to:
- clearly **structure** your writing **using paragraphs**
- use a **wide range of vocabulary**.

To move from Level 5 to Levels 6 and 7 you also need to:
- show **increasing control of a range of sentence types**.

Spelling strategies

Look – say – cover – write – check

Look at the word you want to learn – try to find patterns, learn the shape of the word.

Say the word.

Cover the word with your hand and write it down.

Check your spelling. If you made a mistake go back to the beginning and look carefully at the part of the word you got wrong.

Use a dictionary

Use a dictionary to check the spelling of words you are unsure of. Many dictionaries will also give you information about the roots and origins of words: this is sometimes helpful in learning a new spelling.

Unfortunately, you can't use a dictionary in your exam.

Mnemonics

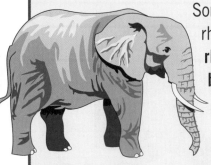

Some people find spellings easier to remember if they make up a rhyme to go with it, for example:

rhythm **h**as **y**our **t**wo **h**ands **m**oving (rhythm).

big **e**lephants **c**an't **a**lways **u**se **s**mall **e**xits (because).

Say the word as it is spelt

Words that have silent letters or unstressed syllables in them are often easier to remember if you sound the part of the word that is usually silent for example:

We**d**nesday, lis**t**en, pe**o**ple.

Break words into parts

Polysyllabic words can be broken into smaller chunks to make them easier to remember. It is almost impossible to spell a word completely incorrectly. Work out which part of a word you find difficult and learn it, for example:

ex – plan – a – tion

KEY TERMS

Make sure you understand these terms before moving on!

- spelling
- grammar
- punctuation
- mnemonic
- polysyllabic

Plurals

■ The following rules will help you with your spelling. However, you need to look out for the exceptions to these rules. Unfortunately, there are quite a lot of them!
■ There are some examples for you to try with each rule. Answers on page 95.

-s -es

Rule: To make a word into a plural add -s.
■ school – schools, shoe – shoes, book – books
If a word ends in -ss -sh -ch -x -zz, add -es.
■ lunch – lunches, glass – glasses, box – boxes
Exceptions: The other rules and conventions on this page show the exceptions to the simple plural rule.

ⓘ *For words that end in a hissing, shushing or buzzing sound add -es. When you say -es plurals aloud you can hear an extra syllable.*

-y

Rule: If a word ends in a vowel then -y, you add -s. If a word ends in a consonant then -y, you change the -y to -i and add -es.
■ toy – toys, key – keys, try – tries, factory – factories

No-change plurals

Some words don't change at all.
■ sheep   deer

ⓘ *The rules for words ending in -f and -y apply when you are adding any other ending.*

-o

Words that end in -o or -oo don't follow set patterns. Try to group words together as you learn them.
■ tomato, potato, mango – all edible and all end in -es
■ tomatoes, potatoes, mangoes
■ tomatoes, potatoes, mosquitoes – they all have toes in them
■ disco – discos, tattoo – tattoos

-f -ff -fe

Any words that end in -ff need an -s to make them plural, for example:
- sheriff – sheriffs, cuff – cuffs

Words that end in -f or -fe are more difficult. Some are made plural by adding -s, such as:
- chief – chiefs, reef – reefs

Other words change the -f to -v and add -es, such as:
- wife – wives, leaf – leaves, calf – calves

Some words that end in -f can be spelled with either an -fs or a -ves plural ending, such as:
- scarf – scarfs or scarves, hoof – hoofs or hooves

 As there is no clear rule, a tip that often works is saying the plural aloud. If you can hear a v sound then it usually means the correct spelling is -ves. cliffs = f sound, calves = v sound

Irregular plurals

Some plural forms don't seem to follow any of these rules and the whole word changes.
- mouse – mice, child – children

You need to learn these words as you meet them.

 Foreign words follow different rules. Learn them as you need them, e.g. cactus – cacti, fungus – fungi.

1 Choose '-s' or '-es' to make these words plural.
bench fox church pupil light wish wash

2 Add 's' or change the ending to make these words plural.
boy fry fly monkey play baby lady.

3 Make these words plural (use a dictionary if you need to).
radio volcano shampoo go

4 Add 's' or change the ending for these words.
wolf knife life loaf roof

5 Write out the plurals of these words.
man woman goose foot

Prefixes and suffixes

- A *prefix* is two or three letters added to the beginning of a word to change or qualify the meaning, for example, dis- mis- pre- un-.

- A *suffix* is two or three letters added to the end of a word to make a derivative of the original word, for example, -ed -ful -ing -ly -ment. Sometimes adding a suffix changes the spelling of the original word.

Suffixes

Adding -ed and -ing

Rule: If the word ends in a single **consonant** and the syllable is stressed, you double the consonant when you add the ending. If the syllable is not stressed, you just add the ending.

- stop – stopped – stopping
- fit – fitted – fitting
- focus – focused – focusing

If the word ends in -e you only add the -d of -ed. You omit the -e if you are adding -ing.

- continue – continued – continuing
- make – making

Adding -ful

Rule: Remember full becomes -ful. You do not change the original word unless it ends in -y (see y ending rule).

- fit – fitful
- hope – hopeful

Adding -ly

Rule: The original word does not change when you add -ly.

- real – really
- proper – properly
- careful – carefully

Watch out for exceptions to the rule, e.g. words that end in -ie: remove the -e and add -y

Words ending in -y or -f

Rule: The rule for adding suffixes to words ending in -y or -f are the same as the pluralising rules.

- fry – fried
- beauty – beautiful
- happy – happily
- play – played
- shelf – shelving

 Learning prefix and suffix rules will help you to spell polysyllabic words.

Prefixes

Rule: When you add a prefix you do not change the spelling of the original word.

- satisfied – dissatisfied
- spelling – misspelling
- necessary – unnecessary

Make sure you understand these terms before moving on!

- prefix
- suffix
- consonant
- root

How many words can you make from these prefixes and suffixes?

Prefix	Root	Suffix
mis	appoint	ment
pre	fortunate	ful
dis	view	ly
un	event	ed
	understand	ing

 Remember: prefixes never change the root word.

Homophones – basic words

- There are many words in the English language that sound the same but are spelt differently and have different meanings. They are known as homophones.
- Many of these words are basic words that are commonly used in everyday writing.

Homophones

The best way to ensure that you get homophones right is to learn them. Some ideas that might help you to learn them are:

- look for patterns
- make groups of words that have similar spellings or meanings
- draw pictures or cartoons
- make up rhymes.

Are: present form of the verb to be, e.g. Where are you going?
We are all the same age.

Our: belonging to us

Hear: to perceive sound, e.g. Can you hear me?

Here: referring to place, e.g. Come over here.

Their: belonging to them

There: referring to place, indicates the fact or existence of something e.g. There is a horse in the field.

They're: short form of they are

Threw: past tense of throw, e.g. He threw the ball.

Through: He went through the door. I read the letter through, from beginning to end.

To: introduces a noun or a verb, e.g. Are you going to school?
I was going to walk today.

verb   *noun*

Too: 1. also/as well, e.g. Can we come too?
2. excessive, e.g. It was too hot. That is too expensive.

Two: the number 2.

Homophones 2

Saw: 1. past tense of see, e.g. I saw you taking it.
        2. tool to cut wood, e.g. Pass me the saw.

Soar: to fly or rise high, e.g. The eagle soared high in the sky.

Sore: painful, e.g. My leg was sore.

Wear: of clothes, etc., e.g. I wear school uniform.

Were: past tense of are, e.g. We are going to school./We were going to school.

We're: short form of we are

Where: referring to place, e.g. Where is it?

Who's: short form of who is

Whose: belonging to someone

 *Make a list. Here, there and where are all place words.*

Make a list

Use this space to record other homophones with which you have trouble. Use some of the strategies to learn and remember them.

....
....
....
....
....
....
....

The word 'there' has many different uses. 'Their' and 'they're' have only one use each. Learn the use of their and they're first; there is used on all other occasions.

KEY TERMS

Make sure you understand this term before moving on!
- homophone

Commonly misspelt words

■ The words on the righthand page are often spelt wrongly. It is a good idea to learn them as they sometimes fail to fit into normal spelling rules.

Word list

Use this page to record spellings with which you have difficulty.

....

....

....

....

....

....

....

....

....

....

....

....

....

....

....

....

....

....

....

....

....

....

....

....

Words that are often misspelt

Word	Rule/Hint
Acceptable	use able if the rest of the word will stand alone – accept
Accommodation	
Achieve	i before e except after c
Analyse	
Assess	
Believe	
Communicate	
Convenient	
Definite	
Desperate	
Disappear	root words never change when you add a prefix
Disappoint	root words never change when you add a prefix
Necessary	never eat cake eat salad sandwiches and remain young
	one collar and two socks
Permanent	
Persuade	
Physical	
Receive	i before e except after c
Recommend	
Responsible	use ible if the rest of the word will not stand alone – respons
Separate	there's a rat in separate
Stationary	not moving
Stationery	paper, etc.
Success	
Surprise	
Weird	a weird exception to the rule!

Don't forget to ...

| Look | say | cover | write | check |

to learn these words!

Punctuation marks

When we talk, we use different tones of voice and we pause after certain words to make our meaning clear. When we write, we use punctuation to make our meaning clear.

Capital letters and full stops

Capital letters and full stops show where a sentence begins and ends:

- the cat was sick in the morning we decided to take it to the vet
- The cat was sick. In the morning we decided to take it to the vet.

Capital letters are also used for:

- the word 'I'
- acronyms: BBC, RAC
- names of people, places and products: Jane, Brazil, Weetabix.

Commas

Commas help us to understand the meaning within a sentence. They are used to:

- separate items in a list
  You will need a pen, a pencil, a ruler and a rubber.

- separate additional information from the rest of the sentence
  John, who was very angry, shouted at the children.

- separate subordinate clauses from main clauses
  When the rope snapped, the climber fell and broke her leg.

  subordinate

  main

- after the following words:
  however, therefore, of course, nevertheless.

Colons and semicolons

- **Colons** are advanced punctuation marks. They point ahead to something which follows. This could be a quotation in an essay or the beginning of a list.
- The **semicolon** is another advanced mark of punctuation. It is used to join two sentences which are very closely linked; this may be where a full stop seems too strong and a comma too weak.
- Semicolons are also used to separate items in a list when they are phrases rather than single words:
  Before you go out you should: tidy your bedroom; wash the dishes; feed the cat and hang the washing out.

Speech punctuation

Speech marks are essential in your writing to show clearly that someone has spoken. There is a lot more to punctuating speech than just speech marks. Here are some basic rules to follow:

- Speech marks "…" or '…' are placed around the words a person actually speaks.
- The first word inside the speech marks always begins with a capital letter.
- The words inside speech marks always end with a mark of punctuation (full stop, comma, question mark or exclamation mark).
- If the sentence is continued after the speech marks (with he said, etc.), then you don't end the speech with a full stop, and the first word outside the speech marks must begin with a small letter.
- If the sentence begins with *He said* a comma must follow this before you open the speech marks.
- When a new speaker begins, you must begin a new paragraph.

For example:

'Tidy your bedroom before you go out,' said my mother.
The man turned and whispered, 'Never ask me that again.'

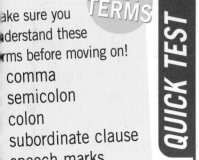

QUICK TEST

Add the correct punctuation to these sentences:

1. shut up shouted james you don't know what you're talking about
2. i want to go home now mum whispered the bored child
3. have you seen my sister asked simon no i haven't seen her since yesterday said Julie
4. i saw james the boy who broke his leg on the bbc news last night
5. when the bell rang the teacher dismissed the class
6. my sister who's a nurse helped to bandage my leg

Apostrophes & paragraphs

There are two ways to use apostrophes:

- **to indicate possession**
- **to indicate omission.**

There are three ways to organise paragraphs:

- **by time**
- **by topic**
- **by talk.**

Possession

Apostrophes can be used to show that something belongs to someone or something. This indicates **possession**.

- John's bag – the bag belonging to John

When something belongs to a single person or thing, add apostrophe and s.

- the cat's whiskers; Sally's coat; the boy's homework

If the word already ends in s, then just add an apostrophe after the s.

- James' book

When something belongs to more than one person or thing add an apostrophe after the s.

- the cats' whiskers; the girls' bags; ladies' coats

If the plural form of a word does not end in s, then add an apostrophe and s.

- the children's homework; the men's hats

It is not just objects that belong to people: emotions, people and actions also belong.

- Susan's anger; Amanda's fear; John's father; the poet's writing

'Belonging to it' does not follow the above rules. An apostrophe is not used.

- its = belonging to it
- it's = it is

Omission

Apostrophes are used to show that a letter, or letters, have been missed out when writing a short form of a word. For example: cannot becomes can't.

If you remember why apostrophes can represent **omission** then you should always get them in the right place.

People often think that the apostrophe goes between the two words that are being joined: this is wrong.

- does + not = does'nt ✗
- does + not = doesnt = doesn't ✔
- it + is = it's ✔

Paragraphs

- A **paragraph** is a group of sentences linked to the same topic.
- Paragraphs help you to organise your work.
- In handwriting, indicate paragraphs by starting a new line and indenting about one centimetre from the margin.

Look at this extract from *A Kestrel for a Knave*. Notice how the paragraphs are organised.

topic

time

Billy tried another rush. Sugden repelled it, so he tried the other end again. Every time he tried to escape the three boys bounced him back, stinging him with their snapping towels as he retreated ....

When Billy stopped yelling the other boys stopped laughing, and when time passed and no more was heard from him, their conversations began to peter out, and attention gradually focused on the showers ....

topic

talk

The boy guards began to look uneasy, and they looked across to their captain.

'Can we let him out now, Sir?'

'No!'

QUICK TEST

Write out the short forms of these words using apostrophes:

do not ....

they will ....

have not ....

I am ....

would not ....

Add the possessive apostrophes:

the mans strength ....

the girls bags (singular) ....

the girls bags (plural) ....

yesterdays meeting ....

Lauras ambition ....

KEY TERMS

Make sure you understand these terms before moving on!
- apostrophe
- possession
- omission
- paragraph

Grammar

Grammar is the way we organise words to make sense.

'This is my dog' is grammatical and it makes sense.

'My this is dog' is ungrammatical; it makes no sense at all.

Parts of speech

Nouns

Common: an object you can see or touch, e.g. pen, table, car.

Abstract: thoughts, ideas, qualities or emotions, e.g. peace, anger, truth.

Collective: one word indicating a collection of people or objects, e.g. group, herd, queue.

Proper: an individual name; a place, a person or an object, e.g. Birmingham, Jane, Tower of London.

Pronouns

A pronoun takes the place of a noun that has already been mentioned: he, she, it, me, you. Use of pronouns helps to reduce repetition in your writing.

John picked up the ball and threw the **ball** to **John's** friend.

John picked up the ball and threw **it** to **his** friend.

Adjectives

An adjective is a describing word. It tells us what a noun is like: **old** book, **sensible** child, **smelly** socks. The use of adjectives in your writing will make it more interesting.

Verbs

A verb makes a noun or pronoun work. There are two types of verb.

Main: as a general rule you can put the word 'to' in front of a main verb, e.g. to walk, to dance, to eat.

Auxiliary: an auxiliary verb helps the main verb, e.g. you **should** walk, he **could** dance, I **might** eat.

Adverbs

An adverb is a describing word. It tells us how a verb is done, e.g. he walked **quickly**, he danced **stylishly**, I ate **greedily**.

Sentences

There are three types of sentence:

1. simple
2. compound
3. complex.

A sentence usually contains a subject and a verb.

<u>My sister</u> <u>runs</u> <u>in the park</u>.
 subject verb   phrase (in this case, information about where it happens)

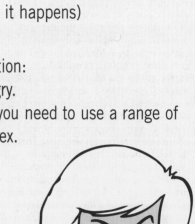

Simple sentences

These give you one main piece of information:

- I ran home. I was late. My mum was angry.

If you want to achieve Level 5 and above you need to use a range of sentences – simple, compound and complex.

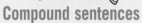

Compound sentences

These are made up from simple sentences joined together by conjunctions – and, but and or.

- I ran home. I was late and my mum was angry but she didn't tell me off.

Complex sentences

These are made up of two or more clauses, one of which must be a **subordinate clause**. A clause has a subject and contains a verb.

Subordinate clauses

Subordinate clauses give background information about when something happened or how people feel. They help you to create two-part sentences. These clauses always begin with words like although, however, because, before. Subordinate clauses can be used in the first or second half of a sentence.

- Although her feet hurt, Jane carried on running.

- The children played outside, despite the fact that it was raining.

main
subordinate

Relative clauses

This is a kind of subordinate clause, which allows you to add more detail to a sentence. They begin with wh- words – who or which.

- My shoes, **which are old and smelly**, need to be thrown away.

KEY TERMS

- simple sentence
- compound sentence
- complex sentence
- relative clause
- subordinate clause
- noun
- pronoun
- adjective
- adverb
- verb

Page 16 Reading fiction

1. Exclamation and question marks (**1 mark**) indicate that they are shouting and there is a lot of disagreement (**1 mark**)
2. Billy is compared to a Jewish child in a concentration camp hurrying towards his death in the shower; because he is thin and dirty he looks like a victim – then what happens to him in the showers is like torture; emphasizes the abuse of power; if Billy is like a concentration camp victim then Mr Sugden must be compared to a Nazi. (**3 marks**)
3. Marks will be awarded as follows: **1–2 marks** (Level 3) for a simple, generalised comment which relates to just one bullet point or repeats the prompts; **3 marks** (Level 4) supports general comment about one bullet point with detail from the text; **4 marks** (Level 5) supports general comment with detail from the text and addresses all bullet points; **5 marks** (Level 6) addresses all of the bullet points, making specific comments supported by explanation and a range of detail from the text; **6 marks** (Level 7) does all of the above, focusing on aspects of language and structure and giving a personal response.

Page 24 Reading poetry

1. Sample answers include: green spears – creates the idea of the nettles as a weapon; regiment of spite – gives the idea that there are lots of them and they are organised like an army of hatred; tall recruits – this gives the idea that the new nettles are the new members of the original enemy army that hurt his son (**2 marks for 1 metaphor and explanation**)
2. "watery grin" shows that he is trying to smile but is probably still crying; if something is watery it is often weak and this suggests his smile is weak and he isn't really happy (**2 marks for 2 suggestions**)
3. The poet feels like the nettles are an enemy army determined to hurt his son and he wants to protect and defend him. Describing the nettles as "green spears" (weapons) and "regiment of spite" (army) shows that he thinks they want to hurt people. He sees himself in battle with the nettles, he attacks them "slashed with fury" until none of the "fierce parade" are left. He continues the metaphor by using images of war to describe the garden bonfire he makes: "a funeral pyre to burn the fallen dead". This suggests he is following the proper, respectful conventions of burying war dead. In the end he knows he can't protect his son from harm even though he may wish to, because soon new "tall recruits" have grown in exactly the same spot. I think the use of war imagery is effective because ... (**1-2 marks - explain what happens with some reference to specific images; 3 marks -imagery identified and commented on; 4-5 marks - personal critical response included**)

Page 34 Reading non-fiction

1. 'Like a beetle walking into a dawn patrol of ants' (**1 mark**) creates the feeling of ambush and surprise; emphasises the feeling of being surrounded and swarmed over; evokes the surroundings of the country. (**2 marks**)
2. effective because it builds up feelings of helplessness and captivity; describes a series of helplessness and captivity; describes a series of basic danger-avoiding techniques she cannot do – frustration and fear; makes us aware of the barriers she faced (**2 marks**)
3. see answer to Q3 in **Reading fiction**

Page 44 Reading media texts

1. Sample answer: Fact - she had been wrapped in sellotape: tells you plainly what had happened to the kitten so you understand she was badly treated. Opinion – subjected to terrifying cruelty: the use of emotive language in the opinion makes you feel sorry for the kitten. (**1 mark for each fact / opinion and explanation = 4 marks**)
2. personal pronouns you and we – creates the sense of 'team' between the APO and the reader; makes it personalised; direct appeal to the reader to help; makes their help seem important.
3. see answer to Q3 in **Reading fiction**.

Page 64 Writing test

This mark scheme will be used to assess your writing.

Sentence structure and punctuation

Ideas and sentences are mostly linked using conjunctions such as 'and', 'but' and 'when'. Sentences are mainly compound. Full stops, capital letters, question marks and exclamation marks are used mostly accurately. (**1 mark**)

Sentences are varied; relative clauses are used. Subordinating conjunctions develop reasons and emphasis. Commas are used within sentences, mainly with accuracy. (**2 marks**)

Compound and complex sentences are used. Phrases and clauses build up detail and give information. A variety of punctuation is used with accuracy. Different types of sentence including exclamations, commands and questions add interest and variety. (**3 marks**)

Shades of meaning are expressed through the use of a range of grammatical structures. A range of punctuation is used with accuracy; sometimes used to create deliberate effects. (**4 marks**)

Sentence structure is varied as appropriate. Simple sentences are used effectively and contrasts achieve particular effects. Punctuation is used with accuracy to clarify meaning and vary pace. (**5 marks**)

Text structure and organisation

Ideas are linked mainly through topic. Points listed in no particular order of importance. (**1 mark**)

Paragraphs generally open with the main idea and contain examples or illustrations. (**2 marks**)

Paragraphs are logically sequenced. There is a sense of introduction and conclusion. Paragraphs of different lengths are used to emphasise ideas or to create feelings of tension or excitement. (**3 marks**)

Detailed content is organised well within and between paragraphs. Some connectives are used to show logical relationships. The introduction and conclusion to persuasion and argument contribute to the persuasiveness of the text. Structure of narrative writing is controlled through paragraph length and organisation. (**4 marks**)

Paragraphs are varied in length to help control ideas. Cohesion of the text is reinforced by the use of a range of linking devices. Paragraph structure is varied to create impact and develop ideas. (**5 marks**)

Composition and effect

The given form of the writing shows some awareness of the reader. There is some relevant content but possibly uneven coverage. (**1–3 marks**)

Writing is generally lively and attempts to interest the reader. A sense of purpose is shown in the content of persuasive writing. In narrative writing the plot structure is clear and is balanced with description. (**4–6 marks**)

Writing is detailed and gives clear reasons for opinions. It engages the reader's interest. A range of imaginative vocabulary is used to describe people and objects. (**7–9 marks**)

A range of persuasive devices is used. Imagery is used in description and alternative narrative structures are explored. (**10–12 marks**)

The tone and content of writing is appropriate and well judged. Narrative writing shows control and development of characters and settings. (**13–15 marks**)

Spelling

Simple words are usually accurate. (**1 mark**)

Simple and polysyllabic words are generally accurate. (**2 marks**)

Words with complex but regular patterns are generally accurate. (**3 marks**)

Most spelling, including irregular words, is accurate. (**4 marks**)

Virtually all spelling, including complex irregular words, is correct. (**5 marks**)

Page 65 Writing test

This mark scheme will be used to assess your writing.

Vocabulary

A linked range of nouns and adjectives are used with little variation for effect.
(1 mark)

Vocabulary chosen to interest the reader and create some effects. Range of nouns, verbs, adjectives and adverbs are used.
(2 marks)

Vocabulary is creative. Adjectives used to compare and contrast subject nouns.
(3 marks)

Range of inventive and creative vocabulary is used to engage the reader's interest.
(4 marks)

Sentence structure, punctuation and text organisation

Sentences are mainly simple or compound. Parts of sentences and ideas mostly are linked by conjunctions. Full stops and capital letters are used with accuracy.
(1–2 marks)

Sentences are varied through the use of relative clauses. Pronouns are generally used consistently, as are tenses. Paragraphs are used appropriately with some sequencing and ordering of detail.
(3–4 marks)

Compound and complex sentences are used, with phrases and clauses being used to build up relevant detail. Punctuation is used correctly. Paragraphs are used appropriately with sequencing of detail. **(5–6 marks)**

A range of grammatical structures is used to vary the focus of sentences. Range of punctuation used correctly. Paragraphs are varied in structure and length in order to reflect the content of the writing.
(7–8 marks)

Composition and effect

Writing shows some awareness of the reader. Although there is relevant content, there is uneven coverage of the prompts given in the question.
(1–2 marks)

Writing makes attempts to engage the reader's interest. Some stylistic devices are used to reinforce the meaning of the piece. The topic is covered adequately, but writing is unimaginative. **(3–4 marks)**

The writing engages the reader's interest. There is a secure sense of purpose. The setting is developed, and various devices are used to communicate meaning. A coherent viewpoint is presented.
(5–6 marks)

The writing engages the reader's interest. Full range of appropriate details and ideas included. Viewpoint of the writer consistently maintained. Good balance between description, information and explanation. **(7–8 marks)**

Page 76 Shakespeare

Some guidance about what is required to achieve each level is shown below. It is not specific to any of the plays you may have studied.

To achieve level 3: a simple retelling of the scenes; some basic features of language identified but no comment; some personal response to scenes but no recognition of Shakespeare's purpose; some recognition of the social or historical context of the play.

To achieve level 4: a few simple comments about the characters; answer still focuses on retelling the scenes; some basic features of language identified with simple comment about Shakespeare's choices; simple comments show awareness of Shakespeare's purpose in the scenes; simple comments on the way social and historical context of the play informs meaning.

To achieve level 5: answer displays a good level of understanding of the characters and their motivation; comments are supported by reference to the text; various features of language identified with explanation and comment showing awareness of the effects of Shakespeare's choices; Shakespeare's purpose and view point clearly identified; some explanation of the way context informs meaning.

To achieve level 6: a focused answer with a degree of exploration of the text; detailed commentary displays understanding of characters, motivation and relationships; detailed explanation of how language is used and how this contributes to character and atmosphere; references to the text are appropriate and relevant and provide evidence of understanding Shakespeare's viewpoint and purpose and the effect this has on the reader; some detailed discussion of the impact of context on meaning.

To achieve level 7: a full answer showing detailed knowledge of the text and the characters; sustained focus on the requirements of the question; detailed and precise analysis of how language contributes to the exploration of characters, motivation, relationships and themes; some evaluative comment about the way Shakespeare's viewpoint and purpose is established and sustained; comments show an appreciation of how specific devices and techniques create effects on the reader/audience; some analysis of the relationship between context and meaning.

Page 81 Plurals

1. benches, foxes, churches, pupils, lights, wishes, washes
2. boys, fries, flies, monkeys, plays, babies, ladies
3. radios, volcanoes, shampoos, goes
4. wolves, knives, lives, loaves, roofs
5. men, women, geese, feet

Page 83 Prefixes and suffixes

Misunderstand, misunderstanding, understanding, understandingly, preview, previewed, previewing, viewed, viewing, disappoint, disappointment, disappointed, disappointing, appointment, appointed, appointing, uneventful, uneventfully, eventful, eventfully, unfortunate, unfortunately, fortunately

Page 89 Punctuation

"Shut up!" shouted James. "You don't know what you're talking about."

"I want to go home now mum," whispered the bored child.

"Have you seen my sister?" asked Simon.

"No I haven't seen her since yesterday," said Julie.

I saw James, the boy who broke his leg, on the BBC news last night.

When the bell rang, the teacher dismissed the class.

My sister, who's a nurse, helped to bandage my leg.

Page 91 Apostrophes

Don't, they'll, haven't, I'm, wouldn't, the man's strength, the girl's bags, (singular), the girls' bags (plural), yesterday's meeting, Laura's ambition

Index